FIND YOUR TELOS

Discover What Orthodox Young Adults & Parishes Can Create Together

Ann Mitsakos Bezzerides & Jenny Haddad Mosher

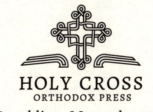

HOLY CROSS
ORTHODOX PRESS
Brookline, Massachusetts

© 2023 Ann Mitsakos Bezzerides and Jenny Haddad Mosher
Published by Holy Cross Orthodox Press
Hellenic College, Inc.
50 Goddard Avenue
Brookline, MA 02445

ISBN: 978-1-960613-01-1

All rights reserved. No part of this publication may be reproduced stored in a retrieval system, or transmitted, in any form or by any means, electronic, mechanical, photocopying, recording or otherwise without the prior permission of Holy Cross Orthodox Press.

Printed in the United States of America

Cover Art:
Mosaic, Empress Galla Placida Mausoleum, Ravenna, Italy.

Names: Bezzerides, Ann Mitsakos, author. | Mosher, Jenny Haddad, author.
Title: Find your telos : discover what Orthodox young adults & parishes can create together / Ann Mitsakos Bezzerides & Jenny Haddad Mosher.
Description: Brookline, Massachusetts : Holy Cross Orthodox Press, [2023] | Audience: Clergy, Youth Ministers, Pastors.
Identifiers: ISBN: 978-1-960613-01-1
Subjects: LCSH: Church work with youth — Orthodox Eastern Church. | Church work with teenagers — Orthodox Eastern Church. | Youth--Religious aspects — Orthodox Eastern Church. | Young adults--Religious life. | Christian education of children. | Christian leadership. | Pastoral theology. | Parish missions — Orthodox Eastern Church. | Christian life — Othodox Eastern Church. | Orthodox Eastern Church — 21st century.
Classification: BX342.6 .B49 2023
| DDC: 281.9--dc23

In thanksgiving for all the people who invested in us when we were young adults

Table of Contents

Preface vii
Prologue ix
The Search 1
Young Adult Needs & Challenges:
Changing How We Think 9
Young Adult Motivation & Capacity:
Changing What We Do 31
Older Adult Needs & Possibilities:
Changing Who We Are 47
Priests and Parish Leadership:
Changing How We Lead Together 57
Becoming A Vibrant Parish:
Finding Our Telos Together 67
A Summary of Reflective Prompts 73
About the Authors 77

PREFACE

A blank canvas can be terrifying and daunting because there is no mark on it. It sits patiently waiting for its first stroke of genius or direction. It can bring about a tension that can stagnate our movements, encumber our thoughts with the fear that our first mark will be misplaced, misguided, and without merit.

A blank canvas can also be liberating because it frees our minds of constraints and opens our consciousness to an endless world of possibilities. It stands ready to accept its first mark, its first sense of purpose. It can reveal a previously unseen beauty of expression and inspire us to think about a subject differently. On its own it may not spark a revolutionary change, but it has the potential to bring about a breath of renewal as it accepts the vibrant colors of dreams and aspirations.

In a way, this was the adventure that was presented to the twelve Telos Pilot Parishes who were chosen to re-envision the way the Church ministers to young adults. We were united in purpose and prayer, imparted with words of encouragement and instruction, provided tools and a blank canvas, and given the confidence to dream.

And so we did.

Courageously and fearlessly, each Telos team began to apply brushstrokes of ideas to the canvas. Each application provoked a new response and over time what seemed like random strokes took form to reveal contemporary vibrant images that only began to convey the many hues of God-inspired grace. Twelve parishes—twelve canvases; countless visions of how to praise God and to minister to the young adults entrusted to our care.

I have had the honor of working and being involved with young adult ministry for nearly four decades and was humbled to be a chosen member (together with our young adults) of one of the original Telos Project pilot parish teams. I was astonished with the insights that all the teams were able to gather through this important and vital research. It has changed the way I minister—not just to the young adults of our parish but to all the members of our community, regardless of their age. I am so thankful to my dear co-workers in Christ, Ann Mitsakos Bezzerides and Jenny Haddad Mosher, for their guidance, compassion and shared dream and I am thankful that the Church may reap the benefit of what we all learned through the publishing of their findings and insights.

As you read through the pages of this book, I encourage you to relish the journey and the opportunity to explore. My hopes for you include:

1. Expand your viewpoint on ministry by broadening your perspective;
2. Embrace the panoramic landscape of the individuals that God has planted in your parish and in His Church;
3. Seek the ability to place young adult ministry in the forefront of your parish consciousness.

I am certain that these strategies will spiritually energize your parish and help provide a renewed vision to your community as it has done for the Saint Barbara Greek Orthodox Church in Orange, Connecticut.

May you firmly establish your feet in prayer, and courageously and fearlessly place your own mark on the canvas provided to you through God's grace.

To Him be the Glory!

Rev Fr Peter J Orfanakos

Prologue

This is a hope-filled book—the hope that young adults have brought us over the last five years about our parishes' potential. It is written for anyone who has ever loved their parish—or what it could be.

The Telos Project, Phase I, was a five-year research project conducted by the Office of Vocation & Ministry at Hellenic College Holy Cross and funded by the Lilly Endowment. The initiative explored how young adults, ages 23–29, and Orthodox parishes engage one another. It was an ambitious undertaking, a crazy idea—and we are so glad we undertook it.

Twelve pilot teams at Orthodox parishes of a variety of jurisdictions, sizes, and make-up from across the country, committed to three years of getting to know young adults, speaking with them about their lives, their hopes, their needs, their faith.

These teams—a mix of young adults and parish leadership—then worked to design and execute ministry that was an appropriate, but often bold, unusual, and creative response to what they had learned about young adult lives and faith. They beta-tested, observed, tweaked, tested again, and experienced exactly what experiments demand—a mix of instructive failures and often surprising successes. Over three years they hosted at least 626 initiatives, engaging at least 647 young adults, connecting them with at least 1,193 additional parishioners.

We cannot thank these faithful folks enough. While it may sound easy to have your young adult ministry funded for three years, we made them work hard!

The Telos teams followed a strictly outlined process that included diligent effort to:

- get to know their young adults;
- build themselves into a functioning team;
- sift what they'd learned from their young adults into ministry efforts they wanted to try;
- craft a clear but simple proposal, complete with a budget, on how to actualize their ideas;
- implement their proposal, reflect on how their efforts worked, and report back to us;
- submit financial accounting and final reflections on their work every year.

Like all parish ministry leaders, they undertook all this work as unpaid volunteers. But there was yet more! Stirred in amongst all of their ministry tasks there were surveys, focus groups, interviews, webinars, online discussions, check-ins, and travel to consultations. And, because we were still "building the ship as we sailed," we often asked them to tack and head suddenly in a slightly different direction. And then, of course, COVID delivered the biggest course correction of all—and hundreds of hours on Zoom.

They did it all graciously, without complaint, and with an incredible generosity of spirit. And they did it while navigating the rest of their lives: teaching kids in public school, filling shifts at family businesses, crunching numbers as accountants, finishing grad school, working as receptionists, caring for patients as nurses and medical fellows, planning weddings, studying for the LSAT and MCAT, traveling as consultants, and caring for newborns. In this way, they delivered precious data we needed, data embedded in fascinating insights, wonderful shared moments, and beautiful new friendships.

This book is a compilation of the most important lessons we learned from them, lessons we feel any parish can act upon.

Despite being written by two academics, it is not written in academic style—on purpose. We've intentionally kept most of the theological content down to only the most essential framing, even as rigorous Orthodox Christian anthropology, missiology, and ecclesiology gave the entire project structure. Similarly, we've kept the facts and figures below the surface; they still shape the course, but don't distract from the horizon. Unless otherwise indicated, all quotes used are taken from reports, reflections, and other written submissions made to us by young adult Telos team members; we've disassociated them from particular individuals and their parishes so none need be concerned about being identified. If you have any questions about the sources of any of our assertions or theological grounding, please reach out; we'd love to share more with people excited about this work and its implications for our parishes!

This book is not meant for a narrow audience of academics, theologians, religious educators or sociologists—but for everyone. It is designed to be a quick, simple, but provocative read—because people who love their parishes are usually busy people: busy in their parishes, busy in their families, busy out in the world. If the story we tell here can convince you to channel even a fraction of your love, energy, and goodwill into a concentrated effort to make your parish a place where young adults are welcomed, loved, inspired to learn, and encouraged to offer their gifts at a new and exciting level, we promise you: we will all be amazed by what God will do.

In conclusion, we repeat: this book is designed to be a quick read and simple, because our greatest ambition is that it would be read, reflected on, passed on to a friend, and then, God willing, acted upon.

As the deacon says at the beginning of the Divine Liturgy: "It is time for the Lord to act." May we all always answer: "Amen!"

Chapter 1

The Search

Young adults step out into the world in possession of new skills and mastery, new perspectives wrought in the crucible of their particular generation, and a powerful drive to apply themselves to something. They are ready for new complexity, new intimacy, new commitment. The question is: commitment to what? Who wants what I know, what I think, what I can do? **Who wants me? Where do I belong?**

The most important answer to that question is: **God wants us.** We exist because God loves us. He created us out of nothing because of his desire to share his life with us. He prepared a world for us so we can grow into the fullness of who he imagined us to be. He sent his son as a pattern for our humanity and to rescue us from death. Whoever we are, wherever we've been, wherever we're going, God wants us.

But it also matters whether humans want us. In infancy, we establish our most primal level of human belonging, that our parents and family want us. In childhood and adolescence, with a widening orbit and deepening explorations of friendship, we begin to separate ourselves from family and to realize and reflect on other relationships—including our relationship with our self. Then young adulthood blooms and, now distinct from our families and increasingly in possession of ourselves, we begin to actively search for who else wants us, for where and to whom we will belong.

Young adulthood is that search. It is the era of finding our tribe and staking out an identity for ourselves—and activating new adult capacities in that quest. It's about surveying our acquaintances, looking for a greater level of intimacy, connection, community; for many, it's also the pursuit of a spouse.

Additionally, as young adults we weigh our personal, educational, and professional experiences, identify where we find the most meaning and promise, and begin forming roots for our life's work (at least Round 1!) We set up households and learn to offer hospitality—first to our friends and neighbors, maybe soon to children.

Young adulthood is when we sift our priorities and make important commitments. Those raised in the Church—and those who were not but are hungering for something more—often decide during this time whether or not they want to be a part of a Christian community. St Paul in his Letter to the Corinthians describes the assembled as Christ's body and then specifically articulates that each individual is a member within it: "Now you are the Body of Christ and individually members of it" (1 Corinthians 12:27). Will all our young adults come to believe this to be true? Perhaps. It depends.

Who wants me? Where do I belong?

When young adults explore these questions and—perhaps inspired by something in their upbringing or brought by a friend—show up at an Orthodox parish, they are looking for a people and a place to belong to. **They are hoping to find themselves in Someone/someone.** And whether or not they do, will largely depend on the rest of us.

Some young adults are looking for God and know it. They may want to build on the solid foundation of a dense and joyful upbringing in the Church, confident that God wants them…but not sure exactly how to find Him now that they have moved away from the familiar. Saying goodbye to a particular expression of the Divine Liturgy, a well-loved childhood priest, a tight and loving circle of family, godparents, and fellow parishioners can feel like a serious and disorienting loss. Or, they may still be at their home parish, trying to transition to knowing and loving God as an adult, but in a community that sees them only as "so-

and-so's child" and assumes their formational needs were met when they graduated from Sunday School.

Other young adults are looking for the love and support of intentional community, something that feels like family, not sure where God fits in. They may be trying to piece together the shards of a more broken experience of church, one through which they glimpsed God and his love, but never in a way they really understood or felt in a sustained way.

Still others may not be thinking about God at all, but are looking for friends of common culture or interests, who might enjoy some of the same things, maybe even someone they might marry and share familiar celebrations and foods, a similar approach to family.

Or, wandering in from the highways or byways, **some young adults may come as mostly blank slates, religiously**, vaguely aware that this fancy building and God have something to do with one another, and that the people in this building claim to care for others. So maybe they'll start their search for God and community here.

All of these young adults should be able to find a place in the Church, because God loves them all. God wants them, just as he wants us who are already rooted in our parishes.

But too often young adults don't find a place in the Church. Too often, the unspoken answer young adults perceive from their parish in response to the question "who wants me, where do I belong?" is an unsettling "not us, not here." When young adults show up on Sunday morning, they can find themselves not welcomed but policed—scanned at the door for "appropriate" dress, interrogated about their heritage or how long it has been since they attended a service, given the side-eye if they sit in the wrong pew. If they walk into coffee hour, hoping to get to know people, they often find all the seats taken by long established regulars, happily chatting amongst themselves.

Other times, a parish does notice and reach out to tell young adults they are wanted, but really misses the boat on what young adults are hoping for when they show up. Eager to attract new members, parishes can be more interested in their own pragmatic survival than in young adults themselves. "We want you" usually means "We want you to help us do exactly what we are already doing. We're so glad you are here, joining our parish community in order that it might survive. Here is the list of the things we need done."

There is nothing wrong with wanting a beloved parish to continue into the future. There is nothing wrong with wanting the next generation to share the burden of its continuance. Most of us mean well. And somewhere deep within us is the foundational understanding of why Orthodox parishes matter.

We want our days to multiply out to more than just our list of tasks. We long for goodness beyond the limits of our weakness, wisdom beyond the limits of our rationality, love beyond the limits of our selfishness. We sense that this world has more meaning hidden within and beyond it. And so we keep coming back to this place of meaning for us.

And in moments of clarity it all converges and we remember: Jesus is the heart of all of this. He is the Author of all this longing, the Beginning and the End of it. So we gather to hear his teachings, to share the eucharistic meal he taught us to eat, to pray the way he and the saints who followed him taught us to pray, and to use those prayers to transform us into conduits for his life and life in the world. We come together to be amazed by and give thanks for what God can do with and through a willing people. An Orthodox parish is a dynamic invitation into life with Christ, together!

This is what young adults need access to, as they emerge into adulthood and themselves wonder how their own days might multiply out to more than their own lists of tasks. They long for direction and meaning and purpose, goodness and wisdom and love. But too often these life-giving understandings, the necessity of our connection with Christ, are buried by our present, much more pedantic concerns about parish maintenance and functioning—and those pedantic concerns are the only things young adults ever hear from us.

And wherever we're at with our understanding and concerns around our parish—its heavenly vision and earthly reality—we need to remember that these understandings and concerns are just that: ours. Our own commitments, however valuable and valid they might be, are not yet the commitments of young adults; young adults did not help craft them and they have no magical access to the experiences, prayers, hopes, and logic that did. Unless we reframe our approach to young adults through their own experiences, prayers, hopes, and logic—where they are in life right now—there is a good chance we will fail to connect with them.

It's hard to express adequately how poorly most of our usual ways of "engaging" young adults line up with their incredible potential and their deep hunger—with their readiness for life, their readiness to give themselves to something, to Someone.

Just when they are able and eager to take on, of their own free will, a truly substantive relationship with God and the Church, we hold young adults at arm's length—or, rather, at the length of our own agendas for our particular parish. **We do this even as we think we are welcoming them in.** And we consistently ignore their very real needs and challenges.

It's time to wake up.

Because young adults and parishes need each other. Not so young adults will have somewhere to get married. Not so the festival can still happen. Church weddings and festivals can be wonderful things, but they are not why young adults and parishes need each other. We don't need each other just to get stuff done. Our relationship is much more essential.

Quite simply, we need each other to grow and live well. Jesus said, "I am the vine, you are the branches. If you remain in me and I in you, you will bear much fruit; apart from me you can do nothing," (John 15:5). All of us are incomplete and unproductive apart from Christ. But that also means we are incomplete and less productive apart from each other. Only when we live in full symbiosis with one another as with all the parts of a vine—loving one another, serving one another, and growing together—will we all yield an abundant harvest.

This book is written to wake us all up. Are you part of the roots or a sturdy stem of your parish? Do you draw in water and nutrients, so much of what's necessary for parish strength? Your commitment and service are, quite simply, an abundant gift! It is now time to inspect the health of your plant. Unless you are connected to young, seasonal growth, fresh new leaves that can take in light from your expanding and evolving surroundings, there will be no adequate transformation of your resources into needed food. And without food, while flowers or fruit may begin to form, they will remain underdeveloped.

Are you a young adult, part of the growing edge of humanity and your community? You are a critical piece of the functioning of this organism. But without a connection to longer established stems and roots, you'll have no way to draw the nutrients you need from the soil. As you unfurl into new environments, the strength of the Vine can support your reach and growth far beyond what you might manage on your own.

Are young adults really this essential to our parishes? We acknowledge: a lot of parishes continue on, sometimes for years, without young adults in the pews. You can exist without new growth for a while. Plants can have regular seasons of dormancy. Sometimes, a fragment of a root that has lain unproductive in the soil for years will suddenly spring to life; the Spirit blows where it will. And similarly, new growth can be surprisingly resilient to hostile conditions, re-rooting elsewhere when it finds itself cut off from the original plant.

But plants that are always dormant are, essentially, dead. And in re-rooting a plant, much time and energy is lost. To live and flourish from season to season, to produce fruit reliably and of sufficient (and increasing) quality and quantity—such that you can nourish an entire community—requires diligent tending of the original stock and new growth. The most incredible vines that produce the most complex and rich wine are those that have been cultivated intentionally, carefully, for generations.

So let's not believe any more that absence of young adults from our parishes is an unfortunate quirk of this age that will correct itself without our attention. Let's not imagine that it will not require all of us to till and prune and weed and water and sow in order to build an incredible vineyard. Young adults are an amazing part of the human family and the Body of Christ; we need them. And they need us. As one young adult reflected:

> *The young adults are the new growth of the church, full of vigor, but in need of inspiration to dream big to carry out the ministry of the Church in the world.*

Where might they find that inspiration? In Christ. In our parishes. In our lives. And even as we inspire them, they'll inspire us.

There has been a lot of murmuring in the last decade or so about the decline and supposed obsolescence of the parish—murmuring that has only intensified in the wake of the COVID-19 pandemic. Much has been written by non-Orthodox authors about whether Christianity has evolved beyond the parish. Some say Christians need to stop organizing ourselves around local gatherings of believers that happen in set places at set times. Some think life has become too chaotic, too overwhelming, too fast-moving for the parish model to work anymore; because we are stuck in the parish model, some say, young adults are passing us by.

After three years of learning from young adults as they try to engage themselves and their peers with their parishes, we've come to a different conclusion. Healthy and well activated parishes are exactly what young adults are looking for—people to belong to, serve with, find meaning and purpose for their lives with—but, most importantly, places in which they'll find themselves in God. Not because the Holy Spirit is not elsewhere, but because parishes were created to be a family of people committed to drawing near to God in worship, keeping the commandments, bearing one another's burdens and producing the fruit of the spirit, loving, and living alongside one another no matter what. Young adults have so many gifts, so much vital energy, such honest and profound inquiry; a parish is the perfect circuitry to receive and channel it all for the building up of the Church and the life of the world.

> *Most young adults I know are not religious. Having a group [of young adults at the parish] reminds me that it's not only ok, but also purposeful to be in the minority of young adults who are indeed religious. Moreover, it reminds me that we are capable of supporting, challenging, and inspiring each other. Having this family becomes all the more important during challenging times, such as being away from home or fighting a pandemic.*

When Orthodox parishes believe they can be this kind of family, and commit to learn how to love and live with young adults, we begin to grow in important ways. What we learn through ministry with young adults starts to spill over into the lives of all our parishioners and into other areas of ministry. It doesn't happen all at once; it takes time, resilience, persistence, and sure help of the Holy Spirit.

But with that time, resilience, persistence, and sure help of the Holy Spirit, your parish can become an incredible organism that dovetails perfectly with young adult needs—and be one of the last social institutions that does.

Chapter 2

Young Adult Needs & Challenges: Changing How We Think

The developmental needs of young adults are perennially the same; the world in which they are trying to meet those needs is chaotically different.

To those of us who are older, young adults can seem full of life, energy, and ambition—and we can worry that parish life is too old fashioned and slow, perhaps too stifling, for young adults at their particular life stage. But the reality is that young adults have many very real needs which parishes have played, traditionally, a significant role in meeting.

Biologically, young adults are living into the final stages of brain maturation, involving synaptic pruning, myelinization of the prefrontal cortex, and limbic system changes; the prefrontal cortex is not fully mature until approximately age 25.

Why is this significant? Because it is only as this physical milestone is achieved that young adults increasingly engage in higher levels of metacognition (thinking about thinking), planning, and abstract thinking. This supports more complex understanding, questioning, and engagement with religious and spiritual realities.

In other words, young adults can contemplate the existence of God in more ways than before. They are becoming capable of cognitively grasping (and actualizing) many of the ideas and practices of spiritual teachers and theologians. What comes before this point lays a critical foundation in faith development, but what comes now is profoundly powerful in its capacity for synthesis and transformative action.

Now, this does not mean all young adults must go to seminary. Entrance to the kingdom of God, Jesus told us, is for those who become like a little child, not the theologically sophisticated. But it does mean young adults will perceive a rift between what they know about God and what they know they have the capacity to know about God, in a way that they did not when they were children.

This is why young adults have so many new questions about the faith and why they've moved beyond accepting rote answers to those questions. This is why, if they remain in a parish as only passive participants, they teeter on the edge of existential boredom or feeling profoundly out of place. The key developmental task of the young adult is to make meaning out of their independent experiences and situate that meaning within a larger context— and then to do something about it. Young adults are wired to process deeply, to craft meaning native to them, to weave that meaning into the world's larger web of meaning and then to act.

This meaning-making and the activity that grows from it happens regardless of whether or not young adults have a religious community. But throughout most of history, religious communities have been fertile soil for both.

In other words, **young adulthood is exactly when human beings are wired to make and commit to a conceptual framework of their spiritual and religious ideas, and then to act on those commitments within the context of community.**

So when Telos Project parish teams began hosting hundreds of conversations with young adults, mapping out where they were in their lives, in their faith, in their relationship with the Church, it was no surprise that they all spoke, in various ways, of a search. Their quest for friends, for a spouse, for a community they would feel supported by and to which they could contribute, their search for meaning and purpose, for vocation, their search for God.

But how they described their lives also showed how their needs and that search have been complicated by **new evolutions in society,** evolutions to which parishes have not yet adequately responded.

What are these evolutions and why do they matter to the timeless reality of life in Christ? Choosing to follow Christ of your own free will as an adult has always included an element of challenge and risk—a step of faith, if you will. It has never been easy. But what we hear from young adults today is that step now happens over an ever-widening gap. Finding one's way over that gap is being made more difficult by dynamics named in various ways by the young adults of the project. We have condensed these dynamics into three chief forces:

- Transience
- Isolation
- Distraction

Let's examine each of these in turn, while acknowledging that, in real time, they overlap and blur into one another. We'll explore the causes of each and how they impact young adults who try to stay connected to parishes. We'll touch on how parishes tend to think about these forces, how it's necessary to start thinking about them differently, and what concrete things Telos teams tried that helped build bridges across that gap.

Transience

It used to be that the place of most young adults in the world—in both geographic and socioeconomic terms—was largely determined by their parents' place in the world. Not so today. While there are still systemic factors that can limit an individual young adult's social mobility, an explosion of other realities allows young adults generally to pursue education, professions, and places-to-live that diverge widely from their family's roots.

While this increase in social mobility has raised the prosperity floor overall, it poses a particular challenge to parishes, especially long-established ones that shaped their ministry around the long-true expectation that people are born, live and die in the same town or city. In the words of one young adult:

> The biggest obstacle to young adults in the Church is our constant relocation. People go away to school, move for work, or start families, etc. and this destabilizes the role of young adults in their parishes. In [our city], being away for an extended period of time can make it difficult to get engaged again, and keeping in touch with everyone is hard. At the same time, seeking out and engaging the young adults who are new to [our city] and haven't been inspired to seek out [our parish] on their own is a challenge.

Human connection (and re-connection) takes time and presence. It's complicated vastly by the pace and scope of serial relocation that many young adults go through in the United States as they pursue education, employment, opportunities, and spouses across the country (or globe). It's hard for many young adults to get comfortable enough, amongst new people, to make substantive connections if they know they are about to move on. And it's hard for them to come home—after having new experiences, growing and changing as people—to folks who assume they are the same as when they left.

> It can be difficult after graduating college to come back to the parish you grew up in and figure out where you fit in as a young adult. Similarly, it's difficult to become a member of a different church as a young adult.

It's also hard for them to figure out where they should serve, if they know they cannot make long-term commitments.

> Young adults crave to find a place in the church but hesitate to take on roles requiring a long-term commitment. Which makes it hard to find out where in the life of the church they fit in.

The challenge is mutual; parishes struggle to love and invest in young adults they fear they are going to lose. "Our young adults" too often means only those who grew up in the parish, whether they are still attending or not (and, ironically, whether we are actively trying to engage them or not!) Graduate students, fellows, interns, and that young adult we don't recognize are just passing through, we think; they are not "ours." Why build relationships with them when in a few months they'll be gone?

The most critical reason, of course, is that we need to love young adults as God loves us—for themselves as they are, not for what they can do for us or because they are already related to us. A close second reason is that the developmental clock continues for young adults, whether they stay in one place or move around the country. They will continue their search, they will make their connections and commitments, they will find their people and their place. But if we resist friendship with a young adult because he or she is not "ours," those connections and commitments will not be made with us; we will not be their people, an Orthodox parish will not be their place.

Further, some day "our young adults," the ones we've raised and love, will be in a community far away from us and we hope they are sought out, welcomed, built up, mentored, supported, and loved by whatever parish they find there. Because the flip side of the challenge of transience is the opportunity to practice the virtues of outreach, hospitality, and encouragement. In the words of one young adult:

> *Hopefully our parishes can do a good job of inspiring young adults to seek out the Church wherever they are and to re-engage with their home parishes whenever they come back. I am one of those young adults who is in flux and have experienced firsthand how easy it can be to fall away. I thank God that I was able to find the Church in my new locale and even take on a leadership position in it. It makes me so thankful to know that no matter where I am, I can depend on the Church to be there.*

The bottom line: all young adults are "our young adults" and we need to think about them that way. We need to acknowledge their need for our investment whether they grew up in our midst or not, whether they are going to stay or move on. And waiting for them to just show up at our parishes or at our prefab young adult events without any effort on our part is not going to work for any but the most motivated—because transience means that young adults are moving too much and too fast, trying to piece together lives in the crazy world we built for them.

How do we address the challenge of increased transience? By being proactive, persistent, and strategic about making sure young adults in your area know your parish is there, that you care about them and their needs, and that you are working to make it easier for them to connect with you.

Telos teams experimented with a number of creative approaches to meeting the challenges of young adult transience, all designed to **make young adults feel more comfortable in a new community more quickly**. You can try some version of them too.

- Attend to the parish webpage as the digital "front door" of the parish; make sure your service times are clear and accurate
- Establish a social media presence for young adult activity at the parish
- Participate in community or campus events that make your parish visible to young adults
- Seek out young adults by having a variety of welcoming events near where they live and work, not just at the church
- Schedule welcoming gatherings to coincide with when young adults might be looking for community or a parish family—when they first move into an area or around holidays
- Offer transportation to church through rides, rideshare credits, public transportation vouchers
- Connect young adults through texting apps
- Attend to young adults' experience of your physical plant; make sure signage is present and helpful,

welcome literature is available

- Provide digital means of buying candles and making offerings (young adults rarely have cash)
- Ensure the people who serve at the candle desk or as ushers provide a warm welcome, an invitation to coffee hour, and clear directions on how to get there
- Support young adults through seasons of intense work, such as MCAT preparation, with prayer, food delivery, study breaks, coffee gift cards
- Help with moves, in or out of town
- Celebrate as "ours" young adult achievements (graduation or match day) and lifecycle moments (engagements or births)
- Talk about all of the above in all parish communications, inviting parishioners of all ages to get involved in your efforts

We cannot reverse increased social mobility and the transience it has created—and even if we could, it's not clear that would be a good idea. Instead, the name of the game is:

- Reach out to young adults even if you know they may only be at your parish for a short time
- Welcome and actively invest in them
- Provide multiple accessible and attractive initial points of connection for them
- Provide supports that help them maintain that connection

Will making efforts like these mean that every young adult who enters your parish orbit becomes a long-term beloved parishioner? No. But if we all wake up everywhere, we will receive into our community beloved parishioners whom other parishes have loved first and we will send on to other parishes young adults we have loved in our turn; we will love our young adults not for our own little corner of the world, but for the life of the world itself.

And don't worry: anything you do for transient young adults will also bear fruit for those young adults who are more firmly planted in your community, strengthening their connections to one another and to you!

> In most instances, it seems like young adults are eager to be part of the life of the church but not sure how to get past the barriers to entry. [....] It's about making a connection, gauging interest, and then taking baby steps.

Isolation

Closely related to increased transience is increased isolation. When we speak of isolation, we are not speaking about mere loneliness. Research has shown that loneliness affects young adults more than any other category of people in the United States[1]—but loneliness is a symptom, not a cause. The cause is a particular sort of social atomization in which we are seeing a systemic breakdown of social ties. People are being isolated into smaller and smaller social units and they are losing the skills and shared experiences that used to bind them together into larger ones.

Isolation has many manifestations, from the replacement of the intergenerational family structure with the nuclear family unit to the intense political polarization being documented all across society. One very real byproduct of isolation? **Increased relational and functional stresses make us wary of and unskilled at making new commitments.**

---

[1] "The Loneliness Epidemic Persists: A Post-Pandemic Look at the State of Loneliness among U.S. Adults", The Cigna Group, Cigna Corporation, accessed April 05, 2023, https://newsroom.thecignagroup.com/loneliness-epidemic-persists-post-pandemic-look.

Most young adults have grown up in a culture of increased isolation; it's why many are likely to be uncomfortable connecting with a new parish in the first place. But it's also why parish overtures that solicit connection—above and beyond what we might have made in prior generations—make sense.

Stop thinking that young adults should know how to integrate themselves into your parish. Don't waste time complaining about how people used to attend church without having to be invited or out of a sense of duty; most young adults have never experienced the kind of social embeddedness or cohesion that made that reality possible.

> Some young adults are timid and need the personal connection and a personal invitation to attend events or get involved with a particular ministry—seemingly the majority are unwilling to just "jump in." After a level of comfort is established, they are then willing to take initiative, seek out opportunities, and proactively take steps to get involved.

And it's not just young adults who have been affected by isolation. Isolation has been slowly deforming the lives of older adults as well. Consequently, it directly affects how young adults experience our parish communities once they find the courage to actually show up.

Young adults very often experience older parishioners as profoundly inaccessible, wrapped up in their own concerns, untrusting or unwilling to give young adults time—even when those older parishioners supposedly know them.

> As I moved from [a city] and am back at my childhood parish, I definitely am met with a sort of déjà vu—the stubborn parish council, people who think I'm home visiting from college (I graduated 4+ years ago), older people not willing to delegate or share leadership roles, etc. I feel like I am back to square one, without a cohort or support system really to encourage me.

Too often, older adults hold the expectation that young adults *should* be persistent in connecting with us, in proving their value, in showing us they deserve our trust, since, well, we were here first. But why should that be so? With that sort of thinking, you will not have any luck with most young adults; with transience and isolation in play, most young adults will move on before you decide they might be trustworthy. As one young adult noted:

> *I really learned that while the Church needs YAs, it takes time and **patience** for the parish (and traditionally older members) to get used to young people being more involved and seeing them as fellow parishioners, rather than just kids. Once that trust is built, young adults really feel accepted when they are genuinely welcomed and known by older adults.*

If your parish is slow to warm up to young adults, you might still be blessed by a few of them who have the patience and resilience to push through your uneven hospitality. But by paying better attention sooner and possessing a real drive to get to know and connect with young adults this pattern can change—especially if you welcome the vision and gifts of key young adults who are willing to help your parish become a more young-adult-friendly place.

> *…[the] trust-building period (for us, it was nearly 3 years!) needs to be spearheaded by a resilient young adult who loves their faith and Church. Perhaps [that young adult possesses]… a certain personality type—a friendly, empathetic spirit who grew up close to their older aunts, uncles and grandparents, etc. who isn't discouraged when met with resistance.*

Intentionality towards young adults by older parishioners—and, hopefully, by the young adults already in your midst towards their peers—is necessary because isolation has inured us all to a kinder, gentler, more socially acceptable form of xenophobia. Whereas most of us would recognize and reject outright xenophobia in our parishes, we are increasingly tolerating a creeping level of isolation.

Take a moment to reflect honestly on how your community conducts itself when a new young adult walks into your bustling coffee hour.

- Is there an intentional and sincere effort to welcome young adults personally, one-on-one?
- Do you work to connect them to others they might share something with (interest, background, profession)?
- Do you make sure they get a seat at a table if they show an interest in staying?
- Are they just left to drift on their own around the edges of the room?
- Do you think they experience your coffee hour as a genuine, shared experience amongst a diverse group of people? Or is it a collection of groups that never mix, always sit at the same tables, and generally resist the integration of new people?

For many of us, the longer we are at a parish and the more at home we feel, the greater the temptation that our interactions with others devolve to a subgroup of people we are comfortable with. One parishioner described it thus:

> [At first, I didn't want to be a supportive adult for the young adult ministry because] I felt like the center of coffee hour would be people [...] coming up and asking me questions. I didn't want to give up my Sunday; I wanted to hang out with my friends at church.

Young adults need us to resist these temptations. Discernment about how and with whom we spend our time is always a key part of our spiritual life—and our own needs for fellowship, refreshment and rest are important. But we should also consider the relationship between attending to our own needs and our love of neighbor. There is a fundamental truth that we know when we have experienced it, for it brings joy: **we gain life when we give it away.**

When we are able to move beyond our own needs, our own kind, to open our hearts and parishes to our neighbors, we fulfill Christ's commands in ways that cause us to grow—as individuals and as communities. Yet it's too easy to miss the neighbors right in front of us: young adults. As one older adult reflected on their experience mentoring a young adult team:

> ...from a pastoral perspective, it is clear to me that many young adults need more personal attention and energy from older individuals than they are often given.

At the other end of the spectrum, isolation can give birth to a kind of comic desperation in our interactions with young adults. With a pattern of declining investment in civic institutions generally, people are giving less time and less money to community groups of any sort, including parishes. Tasks at parishes are often being done by fewer and fewer volunteers. It becomes tempting to view every young adult coming to church as a potential volunteer who can relieve some of the burden of the older generation. (To be fair, young adults *are* potential volunteers. But they are also people worth getting to know, with interests, needs, and fabulous gifts that might not be well-suited to whatever it is we want taken over!)

When parishes feel desperate about their own survival, they often "greet" young adults with attempted conscription into membership or some completely random task. Unfortunately, a common young adult response to this sort of overture is to flee, never to return again. No surprise: conscription is no cure for isolation, but yet another form of it; most often, we are asking young adults to take over something so we can leave or no longer feel responsible for that something.

Building a real relationship that resists seeing someone as a functional part of your agenda is always the better choice. As one wise young adult explained,

> The first step is asking, and gauging what people are/aren't comfortable with. Some people can and want to devote a lot of time to various groups, ministries, projects, etc., while others simply

want to help with one aspect of an event. Accepting whatever service young adults are willing to give is key, and as they become more comfortable they tend to want to be more involved.

Working alongside one another can indeed be a great way to get to know one another, dismantle isolation, and connect as part of something bigger. You just have to make sure that the work you are inviting someone into is work they are comfortable to attempt because a) they feel well suited to do it or b) they feel adequately supported in it even if it is new to them. And you have to care most about whether or not you are actually welcoming them as a new member of your beloved community and not just as a new pair of disembodied hands.

In addition to being thoughtful and patient about how you invite people into tasks, we have to understand the emotional dynamics in play when we invite someone into "our beloved community." Our love for our parish can be so strong and so organic; for us, the stakes always feel high. We care deeply about and feel attached to how things are done. But we have to be careful, because those strong feelings can themselves foster isolation.

We need to know that young adults who walk in the door don't share those feelings. But it's not because they are flighty or neglectful. Quite simply: they don't share our experiences, they don't have long-standing parish relationships, and they have a history all their own. It's unreasonable for us to expect unquestioning reverence from them for our particular established order. Or that they would immediately understand the 90% of parish culture which, like the bulk of an iceberg, lurks below the surface, and navigate it perfectly on the first pass.

If we want young adults to share in the responsibilities of the parish, we have to be willing to share the parish—its story, its identity, its ministries. We also have to believe it has a malleable future, with new life and new ministries on the horizon that must be designed by current and future generations—young people who may not yet know well the Christ who holds us all together, but who need our lives to witness to the importance of a gathered community in His name. We have to recognize that our parishes do not belong to us. They belong to God and are gifted to all of us as a means of glorifying him and making possible our salvation and the salvation of others.

So, how to build something new together? **How do we help everyone, young and old, find their way through isolation and connect more substantially with one another?** Here are the approaches Telos teams tried that worked well:

- Hosting "getting to know you" conversations over coffee, brunch, dinner, drinks
- Sponsoring a food truck as a convergence point for young adults who've come to help set up the parish festival
- Investing in a greater variety of seating arrangements in the parish coffee hour space (creative option: pub-height tables around the edges of the room so young adults can enter and interact at their own pace)
- Posting a prompt or question as a possible conversation-starter at coffee hour
- Running a "Telos Your Story" booth at coffee hour, staffed by young adults
- Offering a "Friendsgiving" event close to Thanksgiving and including casual but structured sharing
- Organizing a professional networking and/or mentoring event, pairing young adults with older adults in the same fields
- Coaching parish ministries on how to break their work down into a diverse array of task and commitment options and how to personally invite young adults to consider joining them

Unlike social mobility, it's hard to see any upside to social atomization. Frankly, it's a force the Church has to resist and you should see your efforts to dismantle isolation and connect with young adults as part of that resistance. Human beings need each other; pandemic-enforced isolation and the resulting mental health and addiction fall-out made that very clear.

The Body of Christ exists because Jesus knits us together from every tribe and nation; relishing the uniqueness of each person God sends us is one of the important ways we live into that reality. Rebuilding our parishes as places where we presume the necessity of connection and are attentive to and generous with one another is a first stage. Disciplining ourselves to pay attention to young adults is the first step.

> *I think that personal connections and outreach remain one of the most effective ways that our young adults feel supported by our parish. Noticing them, knowing their names, asking them how they are, inviting them to coffee hour and events, and integrating them into the parish.*

Distraction

Even when young adults stay put in one place, even when they engage in a parish with a good will, they still face a significant challenge to their ability to make meaning and commitments: the sheer amount of data swirling around them. We are all living within a virtual data hurricane and it is a constant source of distraction and overwhelm, especially for young adults who are still figuring out to whom and where they belong. Author Daniel Pink calls our time the Conceptual Age,[2] an era characterized by heights of affluence, technological advancement, and globalization never before achieved in human history. And it's genuinely dizzying.

---

2   The Conceptual Age is a concept coined by Daniel Pink in his book *A Whole New Mind: Why Right-Brainers Will Rule the Future* (New York: Riverhead Books, 2006), a worthwhile read for a much more comprehensive treatment of this topic than we will be able to give here.

The Conceptual Age is an age of **abundance**, on all experiential fronts: more people, more information, more ideas, more choices, more places, more things—and everything moving faster. Never in human history have there been so many options paraded constantly before us for how we can spend our time, money, and selves, overwhelming our human circuitry (and that's even without considering the addictive and manipulative nature of much of it).

Our newfound state of abundance has raised the standard of living for countless people. Fewer people in the world go hungry or unclothed, fewer people are trapped by their circumstances. We can respond to threats that used to wipe out entire populations with unanswerable tyranny.

But there is a critical price. **Abundance—and the data it generates—creates a landscape in which there is more to navigate; meaning- and commitment-making are made more difficult by the sheer number of dots there are to connect**. This makes young adults' key developmental task—figuring out to whom and where they belong—objectively more difficult than it has been for prior generations. And while a rapid rate of change can be a blessing—when there are diseases we are trying to cure or problems we are trying to solve—a rapid rate of change adds, exponentially, to the sheer quantity of information that needs to be processed **now**, overwhelming our human ability to make sense of a situation.

With this overload of data points, decision-making becomes harder also. Choice paralysis can become a serious factor. But it's not just that a young adult can choose to go to Divine Liturgy or go to the gym on any given Sunday morning. It's that their entire life is abuzz with an undercurrent of decisions that prior generations simply did not need to make because they did not have so many options. And because our human capacity for decision making is finite, the bigger, more important decisions are robbed of the clarity and energy they require by the hundreds of smaller decisions that crowd the field.

However, there is a glimmer of hope in the arena of data overwhelm. **In response to being overwhelmed, the human brain shifts into decision-making by concepts** (hence the term "Conceptual Age.") In other words, so it can sift a more manageable quantity, the brain gravitates towards "the big picture." Unbalanced by too much information/data, **it reaches for those experiences that ground it most in fundamental human reality.**

Young adults experience the Conceptual Age and its distractions viscerally as they try to make sense of their relationship to the Church. They know their experience of being overwhelmed by life pulls them away—and, when given a chance to reflect, know how important it is to return, re-grounding in human experience. One young adult named this beautifully:

> *Everyone struggles to stay connected with the Church. Whether it's in personal prayer or church attendance, the challenges are constant and the most reliable way for me to haul myself back in when I feel myself drifting away is to rekindle a personal connection to a parish member (i.e. inviting someone to an event, asking if someone will be at liturgy, joining morning prayers).*

This impulse to shift away from data, towards concepts and re-grounding in human experience is a necessary reorientation not unlike our resistance to isolation—and, thankfully, it is happening somewhat spontaneously. Human brains are recoiling from data overwhelm on their own. **In the Conceptual Age, all of us—but especially young adults—are reaching out for the fundamental human experiences of empathy, connection, meaning, beauty and story.**

As all the above hints, this is excellent news. Why? Because Orthodox Christianity possesses these fundamental human experiences beyond measure; **Christian love and belonging— empowered by the Holy Spirit, rooted in the Gospel of Jesus Christ and the stunning traditions of the Church— are empathy, connection, meaning, beauty and story** *par excellence.* If this is what young adults are looking for, we have so much to offer!

The trick, however, to offering young adults the possibility of navigating the Conceptual Age via the empathy, connection, meaning, beauty, and story of the Gospel in and through the Orthodox tradition, is that we have to be in possession of that conceptual currency ourselves in order to pass it on. We have to understand Christian love and belonging, practice it ourselves, be open to the Holy Spirit, and be looking for meaning in the story of Jesus and the beauty of his Church. And we need to "surface" all of this so that it is accessible to young adults right alongside the mechanics of parish life. This is one way we make the Gospel come alive for others.

> *...being "known" by other parishioners really made me feel supported. Coming into church and having people intentionally say hello, know my name, and ask how I am doing really made Christian hospitality "active."*

Many already-engaged young adults faltered in their quest to engage their peers because they themselves had not yet grasped "the big picture" of why belonging to a parish makes sense; when they still struggled with finding compelling meaning in Christ's Gospel or beauty in his Church, they themselves became subject to data overwhelm. They found it hard to make good choices about their parish involvement. They found it difficult to navigate their opportunities and options; they struggled to prioritize their Telos work so it happened in a way compelling to themselves and others. And they often recognized themselves what was going on.

> *I need to attend church more often, to make a bigger impact and help the team develop relationships with the young adults. Myself being 29 years old, I am in the target group. My husband and I could benefit from increasing our attendance to church. Since we have gotten married, we have drastically dropped off on how much we attend church on a weekly basis.*

This difficulty is compounded when, looking around, it is hard for young adults to find and learn from a clearly articulated rationale amongst older parishioners for why they should be connected to the parish. Many older adults possess no clear narrative for why *they* give the Divine Liturgy priority over other Sunday morning possibilities, no clearly articulated understanding about the meaning of Christ's life in their own life. They do not know how to "surface" the meaning, beauty, and story of the Orthodox tradition. Instead, when asked why attending church is important to them, too often they will speak of various combinations of duty, nostalgia, or social/familial connections. For example, when asked to share something they loved about church, one adult offered:

> I still see my core [church] friends socially, but there is something special about...seeing your relatives and friends after church [at coffee hour] and not just at a special event.

Meaningful as these experiences are for those who share them, these kinds of rationale prove inadequate for motivating young adults to consistently engage with a parish—because young adults may not have relatives or friends in the parish!

Young adults need more reasons than these to commit. They need something bigger. Why? Over and over again, young adults say clearly what one of them put this way:

> ...[young adults] today are pulled in more directions than any prior generations of young adults. Therefore, if we are going to commit our time and efforts somewhere, we all want to feel that we are serving a purpose.

When our conversations, activities, and shared life with them cultivate not a parochial affection for our parish but an expansive passion for Christ and his Kingdom, young adults' find the inspiration they need for increased engagement with their peers, ministry, and our parish!

> One thing I've learned and continue to learn is about what it means being part of the Body of Christ in his Church. Having brothers and sisters in Christ that share that Orthodox faith and are at a similar life stage is so encouraging and certainly gives impetus to come each week and have fellowship with one another. I am so passionate about Orthodoxy and Telos has been an expression of that passion for me this year as I find my niche within the Church.

> *I hope to help others become more active in the Church through being a part of the Telos team.*

Now, there are some young adults who, even though they have yet to formulate their own strong and clear connection with Christ and the Orthodox tradition, have benefitted from the habits and articulations of their parents. These young adults are able to lean into those inherited understandings to sustain parish engagement and connection while they build and strengthen their own:

> *[We] young adults who have seen the church leadership example by our parents and have actively participated, or moreover led, in GOYA or other similar programs already have an established level of comfort in church programming and leadership and are more likely to "jump in" because [we] "get it"—[we] understand the bigger picture, the mission, the vision.*

But the reality is that most young adults will need help. They will need to lean on the habits, articulations, and inherited understandings of the rest of us while they build and strengthen their own.

So we older parishioners have a lot of work to do—but first and foremost it is work we need to do on ourselves. We ourselves have to remember why we are in the Church, what makes us get up every Sunday morning and put in the effort to help our parish be a vibrant and thriving spiritual home. And then we need to talk about it.

This does not mean that we all will have an identical zeal for the faith and ability to articulate it eloquently. There are different stages to growth in faith that are affirmed in Scripture and different personalities have different "love languages" for our engagement in Church; the way we each frame our love for Christ will and should emanate from the way God uniquely made us. The key is that wherever anyone is at, there is always the intention to seek to grow in an understanding of who Christ is and how participation in the life of his Church increases our capacity for love. It's an ongoing process.

Reflect on your own life:

- What does Christian love and belonging mean to me?
- How is it distinct from love and belonging in the wider world?
- How do we/I seek to practice it ourselves/myself?
- What does it mean to me to be open to the Holy Spirit?
- What is the most beautiful thing I've ever experienced in Church?
- What in Jesus' life compels my devotion?

It's impossible for folks of any age to navigate the Conceptual Age and arrive at Christ without a strong internal compass tuned by a life lived in Christian community. Young adults are still in the process of tuning their compass; who is going to help them find true north? Who helped you when you were a young adult?

If we are going to design and build bridges that will span the widening gap between young adults and parishes, older adults need to be willing to walk with them across those bridges, with whatever practical support, resources, and personal capital they can muster.

But one of the most valuable things older parishioners can do as they prepare to support young adults is dig down deep in their own stories and remember what and who brought them into the fold. There you'll find your motivation, there you'll find your great examples, there you'll find your best practices. Everyone's story will look different, but everyone's story will resonate with the same three things we're going to examine next.

Chapter 3

Young Adult Motivation & Capacity: Changing What We Do

Let us hold fast the confession of our hope without wavering, for He who promised is faithful. And let us consider how to stir up one another to love and good works, not neglecting to meet together, as is the habit of some, but encouraging one another, and all the more as you see the Day drawing near.
— Hebrews 10:23–25

As Telos young adults worked to love and engage their peers in their parishes, we noticed three chief "activities" strengthened their motivation and actual capacity to do so:

- **a community that energizes,**
- **an experience of agency, and**
- **a deepening understanding of their faith.**

In calling these "activities," we are deliberately replacing the usual "activities" people associate with young adult ministry: pizza parties, movie nights, lectures about the faith—in other words, discrete events. Of course, the young adult ministry teams still hosted plenty of discrete events. But the discrete events that built up young adult-parish engagement the most clearly and completely were those that incarnated the "activities" of a community that energizes, an experience of agency, and a deepened understanding of the faith. **These three animating realities are the "secret sauce" that changes young adult activity into something transformative, for both young adults and for the older adults in their orbit.**

None of these factors should surprise us, but understanding them better is worthwhile.

Community that energizes

We've already talked about how young adults have a developmental need for human connection and community. How can we meet that need in the context of the parish in a way likely to engage young adults?

We're dealing with "community that energizes" first because, on the one hand, it's the most common and seems the simplest. On the other hand, it's the one everyone messes up. Because every single young adult ministry builds most of its work around gatherings or "events."

Discrete events are the activity of choice for typical young adult ministry. Many parishes rejoice when they see young adult pizza parties, dances, trivia nights populating the parish calendar; it's a sign that "young adult ministry is happening." But lots of young adult events have an uncanny resemblance to youth group gatherings—just with alcohol now supplied.

And, unfortunately, research is now showing that too often those event-based youth groups don't actually form lifelong Christians.[3]

In the youth group model, someone in the parish decides what they think would be fun or edifying for the young people to do, they organize the details and execute the event. The young people are invited, they do or don't show up, and then they go home. Voila! Ministry for youth and young adults is happening!

However, the track record for this sort of event leading to long-term engagement in other aspects of parish life and to a young person actually being in communion with the Church is pretty

---

3   See Andrew Root's *The End of Youth Ministry? Why Parents Don't Really Care About Youth Groups and What Youth Workers Should Do About It* (Ada, MI: Baker Academic, 2020).

inconclusive.[4] So repeating this format for young adults can prove to be a bit of a dead end.

> *Over the last year, I've realized that an effective team is so much more than simply having the proper communication tools or the right amount of successful events. Being an effective team is more about building allegiance and really connecting with the other individuals on the team. I've realized that it doesn't matter what communication tools we acquire or how many team meetings we have.*
>
> *What matters more is building the motivation that brings Telos young adults back to each other. I realized all of these ideas because of the pandemic. It challenged us to be creative and resilient in ways we haven't had to be before. I don't think we would have been as successful at managing the pandemic had it not been for the heart that we had built in each of our active team members beforehand.*

In other words, the most important thing is community that energizes, community that connects. After three years of Telos work, we now better understand why this is so. The reality too often overlooked is that **hosting events is not the same thing as building community.**

- Events are something one person can convene; communities are only built by people working together.
- People at an event don't need to know each other, interactions are usually superficial; community requires back and forth and the need to communicate more substantively.
- An event is temporary; a community is trying to establish something lasting.

Clearly, building community takes more time, energy, and effort

---

4   See Patricia Snell's "What Difference Does Youth Group Make? A Longitudinal Analysis of Religious Youth Group Participation Outcomes" in *Journal for the Scientific Study of Religion* (2009) 48(3):572-587.

for most of the participants. But that's also why you end up with higher levels of engagement. When people invest in something, with their time, their energy, their thoughts, their gifts, they are more likely to want to stick around to see that investment bear fruit. With community there comes a tipping point where the work to convene becomes so much less of a task because of the joy of the company—the joy of being alongside others you know and love.

Yet despite these vastly different outcomes, we spend far more time, money, and energy thinking about events in our parishes than we do about community.

Now, there is actually a very good and clear reason for that reality. Traditionally, in the United States, Orthodox parishes came with *instant* community—because founders were often related to one another, from the same region, or at the very least spoke the same language and had similar immigrant experiences.

But for most parishes, this is no longer true. Our parishes have become more diverse through marriage, conversion, and the aforementioned swirl of social mobility. Many, many parishes are now made up of people of vastly different backgrounds. In these parishes, community no longer *de facto* exists; it must be built or rebuilt, according to a newly expanded vision of the sort of place the parish needs to be today.

And not just any kind of community. Again, in order for young adults to engage and sustain engagement with a parish, the community they find there and the community they seek to build amongst themselves must be energizing. It must bring added value to their life, or they will go find community elsewhere. Community that energizes is community that connects—with people and with God. As one young adult captured,

> *How needed [are] intentional and vulnerable relationships between members of the church family. As a young adult group we are still struggling to break down the barrier of vulnerability between our members and I believe we learned this year that big social events or organized planned get togethers do not always*

provide the space for growing deeper relationships that have meaning. It is the moments of being open and sharing struggle or life with other [young adults] that creates bonding moments that continue to grow as time progresses. I've found that I truly desire these friendships and am still hoping to find and grow them.

So if you want to help young adults strengthen their motivation and capacity to engage with your parish, you need to stop hosting aimless events and start building community that energizes.

How do you do that? In stages. And to return to our constant refrain, the goal must be to actually supply what young adults are looking for: connection. To others and to Christ.

Now the reality is that "trying to build community" can feel a little awkward or artificial upfront. A number of teams had false starts in this regard, where they declared young adult ministry "open for business" and then, after their first event, couldn't figure out why nobody wanted to come to the next one.

This is commonly what happens when people overlook or underestimate the important first step of building community: **just getting to know folks.** How else will you know what sort of activities they'll enjoy, what they are interested in, what sort of questions they have? Their ambitions, their struggles, their experiences? This information won't just help you plan. It's learning this kind of information about one another that constitutes relationship building, that creates connections. And it is relationships which make it possible for us to know who is in our community—their gifts, their ideas, their actual capacities—and thereby attend more carefully to the task of building a community that energizes.

This is why Telos asked teams to begin their work with what we called **empathetic conversations**, structured but casual gatherings, the only goal of which was to listen to people's stories, where they were in life, and get to know them and their real needs.

Don't skip this step. And don't think if you do it once, you will never need to do it again. The reality is that empathetic conversations with young adults need to be part of our regular habit of interaction with them because they and their world keep growing and changing. As an example:

> *My favorite moment from Telos this year happened in January. Our work was suffering from a large amount of turnover in the leadership and general disinterest. We were losing our young adults and it was frustrating to many people on the team, which only further worsened the disinterest. But we decided to host a Vasilopita dinner with no agenda other than to bring people together again. It turned out to be very successful, and it seemed that both leadership and general participants in the group were excited to start fresh again.*

Once you do have a sense of folks and what makes them tick, then it is time for the relationship and community building to begin in earnest. Based on young adults' expressed interests and needs, Telos teams designed a wide spectrum of activities for young adults, which, as they evolved, mostly fell into the following buckets:

- Fellowship
- Faith Deepening
- Service/Outreach
- Intergenerational relationship building

On the outside, these all might look like regular young adult ministry sorts of activities. But again, what mattered was the animating reality on the inside.

- All were designed in direct response to an interest or need expressed by young adults
- All were planned by young adults themselves; older adults played an entirely supportive role
- All sought to connect young adults with one another, with young adults elsewhere, with older members of

their parish, with community neighbors, with their priest, with Christ

- Creativity, boldness, and out-of-the-box thinking was encouraged; it was okay to fail
- Participants were asked to give their feedback on the activity, the team reflected on their responses together and then moved on with the lessons learned to improve their next activities

There's another hidden benefit to this approach. By starting with a team, rather than a single young adult leader, you immediately have the nucleus of a community of young adults. Ideally, your team will function as an energized community in order to get the event to happen. And therein you have already won half the battle. You have a small group of young adults excited and interested in working together to serve their peers and setting an example of energizing community for the rest of the parish; as a young adult shared: "Not enough of a crowd to be scary, but enough to be fun." And like attracts like.

Some may criticize the act of getting input from young adults and allowing them to design their own ministries as a consumerist approach to church activities. It is much more fruitful to think about the process as building ministry around real people, actively drawing on the best Orthodox missionary ethos of real enculturation.[5] And it *de facto* creates a series of connections.

- The team connects with the young adults, asking about their lives
- The young adults reach into themselves and connect with their own stories and their own interests and experiences of God as they bring them out to share with the team

---

5   For more about the Orthodox missionary ethos of enculturation, see Archbishop Anastasios Yannoulatos' *Facing the World: Orthodox Christian Essays on Global Concerns* (Geneva: World Council of Churches, 2003).

- The team plans an activity, connecting with one another on various points as they figure out how to plan something worthy of the interest and the person who offered it
- The planned activity then shares that interest amongst the wider group of young adults, connecting them with one another, and giving them a new point of connection in their further interactions with the wider parish and with Christ

Community that energizes is community that connects. It's engaged, active, reflective, vulnerable, and responsive. It encourages people to remember who they are and what they care about, to get to know their neighbors, to celebrate those things that make each of us unique and which add more beauty and interest to the whole. Finally, it grants agency in accordance with people's God-given gifts and personal capacity.[6]

And the more connected the community of the Body of Christ is to one another, the more clearly we will see Jesus and the more energized we will be for the work we have to do together. As one youth and young adult minister reflected:

> I've learned that in my own Church work, ministry should be as organic and relationship focused as possible. It is very easy for ministry to become institutionalizing and programmatic which seems to be a sure fire way to lose involvement.

Experience of agency

The opportunity to initiate, design, and execute something yourself, without fear of micromanagement or failure, is the second necessary "activity" or animating reality of young adult ministry. Cast your eye back along all the discussion of community

---

6 To dig more thoroughly into the mechanics of community that energizes (and, conversely, community that de-energizes!), see Liz Wiseman's *Multipliers: How the Best Leaders Make Everyone Smarter* (New York: Harper Business, 2017).

that energizes and note particularly the strong theme of this—what we understand as the *experience of agency*.

Agency is how we step into and become ourselves. Infants are dressed by their parents each day; seeing a baby in a particular outfit gives us no indication whatsoever of their personality. But once a child begins to choose clothes for themselves, all of a sudden, a personality emerges! Similarly, when a child is taken to church every Sunday by its family, their presence is not an expression of their own piety. But once a young adult can choose whether or not they attend church, what kind of a church, how often, what kind of services, suddenly the spiritual realities that have been swirling in their heart emerge and begin to take concrete shape as their own decisions, commitments, beliefs, and practices.

Agency is not inappropriate willfulness; it is the expression or realization of a person whom God created. It is exactly what should be happening in the lives of young adults.

And we know this because young adults are exercising agency in all other areas of their lives; that's one definition of being an adult, after all. Young adults are purchasing and managing property. They are setting and meeting budgets. They are embarking on professions that might have them saving lives, shaping youth, arguing in court, analyzing critical data. So why is the parish the one place they are treated like children?

Within the Orthodox tradition, it is clear that personal maturity is a desirable feature of leaders. Indeed, in the canons, some forms of leadership are reserved to those of a certain age. And yes, agency can be misused; we call that sin. But before we allow these thoughts to scare us away from letting young adults exercise agency, we must know: without the exercise of agency, there can be no virtue. So if we want young adults to practice virtue, to become ethical and moral adults, we must give them opportunities to act freely in parish life.

> As a young adult it's difficult to be an engaged member of a church community, but being part of a leadership team adds an element of responsibility that encourages participation and accountability.

In the presence of discerning oversight from their priest and encouragement and advice from other parish leaders, lack of personal or spiritual maturity is never a reason to refuse to give young adults responsibility, because responsibility is exactly how they will grow. Telling a child how to tie a shoelace is no substitute for actually coaching them through the motions of it, as painfully slow as it can sometimes feel! In order to learn how to do it, they have to be allowed to try it.

If we force young adults to sit on their hands, how will situations arise in which they seek necessary perspective and feedback and answers about life in the Church? How will they practice Christian leadership in ways that will help them improve? How will they feel like they actually belong as a needed and necessary part of the Body?

> I think young adults feel most connected and supported when they are filling a role or a need of the parish, and members of older and younger generations express gratitude. ...Young adults today are pulled in more directions than any prior generations of young adults.
>
> Young adults feel most connected and supported by our parish when the parish gives us the chance to take the lead. This has been the case with our Bible Study (which is entirely led by young adults) and by our [...] lecture last year. There's a certain level of trust involved in endeavors like these that is very validating when the outcome is so positive.

Let them lead now. If yours is a new young adult ministry, you can set up, in consultation with your young adults, a commonly agreed upon system that helps keep everyone informed and mutually accountable. But don't place burdens or expectations on them that you do not place on ministries run by older parishioners.

Further, don't restrict them to just leading young adult ministry. In healthy parishes, young adults will begin to flow from leading among their peers to leading in other ministries. In every single case that we know of, this was experienced as an extremely positive development. Don't miss the chance to pair young adult gifts and energy to all different areas of your parish ministry.

> *I believe the young adults fit into every aspect of the life of the Church from participants to leaders to mentors to mentees. The key is finding a role for each young adult in which they feel comfortable and can succeed. We are fortunate to have a community that not only accepts, but seeks out the knowledge and assistance of young adults, it just takes some time to find the right fits.*

Again, young adult leaders will occasionally need help and guidance from other parish leaders. They will sometimes make terrible mistakes. They will sometimes manifest immaturity. In reality, that makes them no different from older adult leaders in our parishes.

Further, giving young adults agency often results in them desiring to know and understand established wisdom; they begin to marvel at and admire the work and sacrifice generations ahead of them have made, to aspire to a similar sort of sacrifice in their own turn.

In sum, if we give young adults the chance now, to join us in building something real, we'll reap the fruits of that harvest together for decades to come.

Deepening understanding of the faith

Finally, as we shift now to the importance of deepening understanding of the faith as the final "activity" that strengthens young adults for engaging with their parishes, we want to frame what we are about to share with a critical observation. Notice we are giving faith deepening special attention here, all the while it is also one of the four key buckets of young adult ministry: fellowship, faith deepening, service/outreach, and intergenerational relationship building. **By giving it attention here, we must simultaneously caution that you *not* consider it universally more important than all the others, for all young adults, at all times.** One young adult made this observation based on the team's practical activity:

> Finding a balance between the spiritual and communal offerings of the Church is probably the key to ensuring that young adults stay engaged in its true form.

We are reminded of the story of Abba Anthony:

> A hunter in the desert saw Abba Anthony enjoying himself with the brethren and he was shocked. Wanting to show him that it was necessary sometimes to meet the needs of the brethren, the old man said to him, "Put an arrow in your bow and shoot it." So he did. The old man then said, "Shoot another," and he did so. Then the old man said, "Shoot yet again," and the hunter replied, "If I bend my bow so much I will break it." Then the old man said to him, "It is the same with the work of God. If we stretch the brethren beyond measure they will soon break. Sometimes it is necessary to come down to meet their needs." When he heard these words the hunter was pierced by compunction and, greatly edified by the old man, he went away. As for the brethren, they went home strengthened.

A healthy life requires balance. Support your young adults as they design opportunities to both pray and play; you'll be coaching them in how to use their agency to build a sustainable community life.

Additionally, recognize that even older adults in the church vary widely in their capacity and interest for theological discussion or knowledge. We all generally accept this as a normal state of affairs. Some people come alive with elaborate theological insights and could discuss them for hours; others thrive on straightforward life applications and are often moved more quickly to action. The Church has always contained people of varying levels of education and capacity to articulate theology.

It would be unfair and inappropriate to try to enforce some kind of standard across times, cultures, literacy and education levels, expecting all adults to know all the same things about the Orthodox tradition.

So it is important to be clear: when we talk about deepening understanding of the faith, we are not talking about amassing knowledge. We are speaking about deepening understanding. Deepening understanding means that, wherever you start, you go deeper. You end someplace where you have built more meaning for yourself than before you began. The end goal of deepening understanding of the faith is a lived Christian wisdom. And we know this kind of wisdom can be found both in a loving grandparent who never learned to read and in the learned theologian who translates from original texts.

Deepening understanding is something young adults are doing constantly in all areas of their lives; as we touched on earlier, it's the outcome of the final stage of adult brain development, the natural exercise of true adult capacity. They are doing it at work, they are doing it in their friendships, in their romantic relationships, in their relationships with their neighbors. It is a developmental task of the age.

So if the one place young adults are not deepening their understanding is at church, we have a serious problem: the parish is not meeting young adults' need to use their new, expanded capacity for learning in conjunction with their faith.

The uncomfortable truth is that between whatever level of religious education a young person receives in the church and their capacity for learning when they launch into the world as a 22-year-old, there is almost always a significant gap.

What does that mean? It means that when you consider the intellectual, spiritual, and psycho-social capacities of a 22-year-old young adult, they will already be "behind" in terms of their religious education. They have the capacity for more than they have been provided.

To test the truth of this, compare what any 18-year-old knows about a subject they study during senior year in high school to what they know about the Orthodox faith. Except for a very small subset, for most there will be a huge disconnect in quantity, quality, and complexity of knowledge.

Repeat this exercise for every year between 18 and 22 and the disconnect becomes greater, except for those who go on to formally study their own tradition.

Finally, arrive in young adulthood proper and, with final brain maturation at approximately age 25, a new suite of spiritual capacities is now complete and ready for use…but will likely go unused.

Why unused? Because the young adult already feels so "behind" that he or she feels too embarrassed or awkward about trying to catch up. Because adult education opportunities are so few in many of our parishes. Because those opportunities that do exist are offered on a schedule that suits retirees, not working young adults or graduate students.

And so the problem compounds.

Universally across our research, young adults who grew up Orthodox shared that they feel inadequately prepared to function as Orthodox adults religiously or spiritually—and it is largely a byproduct of the process described above.

Orthodox young adults know Orthodoxy has played a significant role in their family history, but they don't understand the significance of it in their daily life. While they may have treasured memories of church life and people or affection for particular Orthodox traditions, they can feel like they've missed "the big picture" about being Orthodox Christian—what does it mean, what is it for—especially in a pluralistic society where most are not Orthodox?

They also may have particular questions about Orthodox theology and how it intersects with contemporary issues and concerns. But they feel ill equipped to answer those questions themselves and feel awkward about seeking answers from others. They wonder: shouldn't I, at my age, know more than I do? A Bible study or a book group might sound interesting…but will everyone there know more than I do? Is that my own fault?

As a result, the young adult's relationship with Christian tradition starts to feel frustrating, restrictive, and increasingly unsatisfying. And not just in terms of the life of the mind and questions of doctrine. Drop them into a long church service, packed with the riches of a tradition mostly inaccessible to them, and they can feel completely at sea. As far as they can tell, they've been left to try to meditate on their own for three hours against a background of nonsensical hymns—and it's a tough recipe. It is not unreasonable that a young adult kept in this state of unlearning will eventually come to believe that there must be nothing else to learn.

Of course, nothing could be further from the truth—and not just for young adults. Learning about your faith is a need common to all Orthodox adults—but it is of pointed significance in young adulthood. Remember the search! A young adult trying to build a model for their life is hoping to use pieces from all arenas of life. If there are no pieces available to them about faith, the model will be built without it.

And that is a tragedy. Because deepening our understanding and experience of the faith is not just about protecting us from frustration with the Church or preventing a negative impression of the Orthodox tradition. It's about supplying us with the rich food we need to sustain us through the challenges of adult life.

Young adults need to know how tenderly the scriptures speak of God's love for his people—and for them. They are hungry—and ready—for the clarity and challenge found in the teaching of the prophets and the preaching of Jesus. They should experience the deeply moving wonder of reading the Psalter at Christ's tomb on Holy Friday night. The felt presence of the saints in their lives, as both hope and help, is vital. What if, when their first child is born, they do not know the Church already has a blessing for him or her on the very first day? They deserve to be shaped, as we have in our turn, by the knowledge of the depth to which God is with us, in solidarity with our lives, even into and through the grave.

Why should a young adult, searching for sustenance for their life, for answers, for meaning, for resonance, be deprived of this ancient abundance? What else will provide them even a fraction of the depth, perspective, wisdom, and time-tested truth of the Orthodox tradition? What else will provide Christ? And in Christ, the River of Life floods its banks and never runs dry. We will always have water for our souls.

Young adults need this sustenance. They need it for life and they need it if they are going to stay connected to the Church. An older adult might continue in the Church through a spiritual dry spell out of habit or supported by already established relationships; a young adult has not yet established habits or relationships and so is much more likely to simply go elsewhere to find community, practices, and beliefs that can give their life meaning, in an honest attempt to survive the drought.

CHAPTER 4

OLDER ADULT NEEDS & POSSIBILITIES: CHANGING WHO WE ARE

The gifts Christ gave were that some would be apostles, some prophets, some evangelists, some pastors and teachers, to equip the saints for the work of ministry, for building up the body of Christ, until all of us come to the unity of the faith and of the knowledge of the Son of God, to maturity, to the measure of the full stature of Christ. — Ephesians 4:11–13

We've spent considerable time discussing the needs, capacities, challenges, and motivation that all intersect for young adults when they try to connect with a parish. We're now shifting gears to speak about **the explicit needs and challenges of individual older adults and how those relate to young adult ministry**.

But…surprise! This chapter is not about parish council members, professional young adult ministers, or the priest. This chapter is about "everyone else"—the older lay adults in a parish.

Because while "everyone else" may have no formal or professional responsibility for young adult engagement in a parish, we do have a critical role to play. And it is a role that, when fully and faithfully lived into, will benefit not only young adults but older adults also.

Just like "the search" of young adults, all older adults have our own developmental task. Our brain development may be complete, we may have achieved a level of social, intellectual, and spiritual integration that young adults are seeking—but we are still growing. We still have an important developmental milestone to achieve: generativity.

Generativity is the critical move beyond preservation of the self.[7] It is the key task of middle adulthood (approximately ages 40–65). Generativity is what we build in ourselves when we use the capital accumulated in younger adulthood—our emotional, intellectual, spiritual, psychological, social, and even material resources—to contribute to the building up of something beyond ourselves.

Generativity is part of what is going on in the experience of parenthood, in the pursuit of a career, or our long-term commitment to a cause. The tools of generativity are care, commitment, investment, and mentoring. We look to create something that will outlast us by investing in the people who will come after us…and that act of creation in turn has a deep impact on us, changing and forming us into better versions of ourselves.

Generativity should also be part of how we think of our role vis-à-vis young adults in our parishes—even when we are not their parents or grandparents. Because generativity is an important dimension not only of developmental maturity, but of spiritual maturity. Older adults are also called to grow up into the fullness of the stature of Christ—and they need young adults to help them do it.

If you are an older adult, you need young adults in your life. And your parish needs young adults woven into all aspects of

---

7   The concept of generativity was first identified by Erik Erikson. For more on Erikson's original research on generativity, see *Vital Involvement in Old Age,* by Erik H. Erikson, Joan M. Erikson, and Helen Q. Kivnick, (New York: W. W. Norton & Company, 1994). For a more contemporary exploration of generativity, see Arthur C. Brooks' *From Strength to Strength: Finding Success, Happiness, and Deep Purpose in the Second Half of Life* (New York: Portfolio, 2022). And finally, James W. Fowler's book *Becoming Adult, Becoming Christian: Adult Development & Christian Faith* (San Francisco: Jossey–Bass, 1999) is a classic exploration of how developmental stages intersect with faith.

its life. Not so that there is someone to show up to unlock the doors when your custodian finally gets too old and not so that there will be a next generation to pay the bills. But because you and your peers in the parish—whatever roles you fill, whatever ministries you are a part of—cannot grow up into the fullness of the stature of Christ without them.

What do we, as individuals, actually need from young adults? **We need the humbling opportunity to share our stories, our lives, and our faith with them.**

We need to come alive by getting to know young adults, reflecting with them on their challenges, joys, adventures. In this process, we might realize we have some hard-earned wisdom that might be useful. Or we might realize that just presence with and alongside young adults is all that is needed, much in the way a toddler needs a parent to watch them learn to walk on their own. The parent can't really *teach* a toddler to walk or share wisdom about walking. But the parent can be near, there with an excited nod when the toddler takes a few tentative steps; and a yelp of encouragement when it's a lot.

Given all the realities of our world today, it's helpful to hold this mindset: **when a young adult shows up to church of their own accord, you are bearing witness to a miracle.** In Chapter 1, we named all kinds of reasons young adults may come to church. At the most basic level, we know there is some instinct to pray and some instinct to connect. It's this connecting where older adults play a vital role. Because all young adults today are struggling with isolation, distraction, and transience, what they need from older adults is welcome to a sense of community, presence of being, and assistance in developing a sense of place. We're going to talk about how we share our faith with young adults, but before we even get there, we want you to know that even if you have never ever shared your faith with anyone, you can still be extraordinarily key in the lives of young adults.

Individually, here's how anyone and everyone can help:

- If you're sitting in a pew near a new young adult, and it's appropriate at the end of the service as people are in line to receive a blessing from the priest, turn to them and introduce yourself, perhaps asking, "Are you new to the area?" if you are sure they haven't been coming for weeks. Invite them to come to coffee hour with you.

- At coffee hour, approach a new young adult in a friendly (not in-your-face) way to welcome them—ask genuine, kind questions to find out more about them.

- In the following weeks/months/years, check in with them at coffee hour as you might your own niece or nephew, or a junior colleague. How was their week? What are they excited about at work? Share a story about your own life—what are you learning that's worth sharing? What's something that you wonder about that their perspective would be interesting on? Don't feel like you need to provide any grandiose advice: a curiosity and appreciation for their life and context, whatever is going on in their life, and telling stories about yours, are often helpful in ways you cannot anticipate. For a young adult, they feel seen and heard, and welcomed to get to know you.

- Invite them to work alongside you for parish tasks that bring you joy, and get to know them in the process.

- Invite a group to your home for a meal who might benefit from getting to know one another more—and be thoughtful about the conversation.

At all times, be attuned to their interest in conversation with you. Don't push it—but you should be able to sense if they want to talk more. If they connect with their peers and develop or join a robust young adult group, that's wonderful! If that does happen, don't let them feel siloed off from the rest of the parish—check in on them regularly and warmly! And if that doesn't happen, it doesn't mean your parish isn't a place young adults can thrive—they may be showing up precisely because they need an intergenerational community of people who care.

Know what's going on at the parish for them, invite them to wider parish initiatives, or important offerings that they can access if needed. For example, if they mention struggling with big questions or seem troubled, make sure you help connect them to your priest.

All of this is just simple human-to-human interaction. You are letting the parish community become a wider family for young adults—people to check in with, hear a perspective from, be encouraged by. You do not have to feel comfortable talking about your own faith, Christ and his Church, to play a vital role in connecting young adults to your parish. You just have to show up and be warm and loving—and they will see, in and through who you are, what a life of Christian commitment looks like.

This said, we want to spend the rest of this chapter convincing you that it's worth trying to share your faith verbally with young adults, because we also know that when adults are able to talk about Christ and his wisdom—gently, authentically, and without politics or polarization, it has a remarkable impact on young adults.

Most of us don't do this. Sharing faith with young adults can seem out of our league for the vast majority of us who are not formally trained religious educators, young adults ministers, or priests or pastoral assistants. Why?

First, **we don't feel adequate to the task of sharing our Orthodox Christian faith with others.** Many, many Orthodox laity feel that the understanding they have of their own faith is partial and somewhat personalized. Their faith serves them well enough for them to adhere to it, but they feel wholly unready to share it. They might even feel like they need permission to share it.

There are several historical and cultural reasons for this state of affairs, but the outcome is that, for many laity, there is something about cultivating young Christians that feels like it should be left to the professionals. In sum, the Orthodox tradition is vast and complex as a body of knowledge; what if we mess up the transmission of it?

And second, **young adults are cool, but kind of scary.** Their world is very different from our own, swirling with big and difficult questions. What if we cannot answer them? What if there are no easy answers? What if we are shown to be wrong?

Because the need to be generative is so critical to our own wellbeing, the wellbeing of young adults, and the wellbeing of our parishes, these are insecurities we need to get over. Young adults are not, in general, coming to us for information about Orthodox faith. The internet has that in abundance—so much so, in fact, that it can be profoundly confusing. Instead, in order to make sense of all that information, they are coming to us to grab hold of those conceptual handles we spoke of earlier. They are coming to us for our empathy and for our concrete experiences of the stories, images, beauty and poetry—the truth—of Orthodoxy at work in our everyday lives.

We are not here to be their spiritual parents or their gurus. We are not here to replace the priest, who, as we're about to explore in the next chapter, has his own unique role. We are here to be loving older brothers and sisters, aunts and uncles in Christ. They may indeed sometimes have questions we cannot answer—but that is fine. What better moment to model where and to whom we go for answers? Or how to carry on in faith in the midst of ambiguity?

Christ's final instruction to his followers was to "Go therefore and make disciples of all the nations, baptizing them in the name of the Father and of the Son and of the Holy Spirit, teaching them to observe all things that I have commanded you" (Matthew 28:19–20). This is core to the Gospel: to be a follower of Christ is to pass along to others what you have received—

your understanding and experience of faith, hope and love in and through Christ. It is a fulfillment of the instruction to the Israelites to teach their children the Lord's commandments: "You shall teach them to your children, speaking of them when you sit in your house, when you walk by the way, when you lie down, and when you rise up," (Deuteronomy 11:19).

Now, note that the description is not of the commandments being passed along via lectures or formal classes, but via shared, everyday life. "Making disciples" is the Church's version of generativity—because only by helping form followers of Christ can we ourselves live into the fullness of Christ's own life.

To live as a Christian is to imitate Christ; Christian means "little Christ." When we pray to our Father, we imitate Christ's own prayer. When we fast, we imitate Christ's own fasting. When we study the scriptures, we imitate Christ's own attention to those same scriptures. When we feed the hungry or care for the sick, we recapitulate what Christ himself did via miracles and thus perpetuate his love and care for humanity.

But what of Christ's instructions to "make disciples"? Each of us needs to discern what that looks like for us, based on our abilities. The best means of discernment is to read and reread, hear and re-hear the Gospels, attuned to how Christ shared life with his own disciples, asking ourselves the question as we do: What does generativity in the church with young adults look like? Here are a few ways in which we share faith:

- Modeling for them how to observe the commandments by keeping them ourselves, to the best of our ability
- Engaging them in deep conversations about the realities of life
- Exploring with them the ethics and value of their work
- Sharing stories of your own life where your faith in Christ held you together in the midst of struggle

- Exemplifying how to be with all kinds of people, even as others criticize us
- Serving them—or with them—at parish meals
- Granting them our time and attention (in what can sometimes seem like disproportionate amounts)
- Explaining things to them on a deeper level than we might explain things to others
- Entering into hard conversations with them, being willing to draw on your best insights about life lived wisely
- Being patient with them, sustaining your relationship with them through mistakes, misunderstanding, offense or non-agreement
- Discovering the world with them via study or on pilgrimage
- Praying for them
- Teaching them how to pray
- Inviting them into the communion line with or even ahead of us

As an older adult mentor observed:

> ...the [young adults] who [the older adults] did stay close to and involved in their daily lives seemed to have the strongest experience of God's presence and commitment to His Church.

When we do any of the above things with and for young adults, we are living into the generativity that we need to be fully human and to be a disciple of Christ ourselves. Because these are the ways Christ made disciples. And if we fail to make disciples, we are failing to imitate Christ in all things and in achieving His real end.

Christ's miracles were never the real end, or *telos* of his ministry. Everyone Christ raised from the dead during his earthly lifetime eventually died again. No, Christ's miracles existed for a purpose outside of what they concretely achieved in his earthly lifetime. The actual goal was the transformation of the Twelve and the others who would then become teachers and witness to many more. The real *telos* was the Church, a community of believers, filled with the Holy Spirit—and through the Church a restored humanity, living into the glory of our original design.

Christ made disciples of people of all ages—and so should we. Intentional investment in a new follower of Christ is needed whatever the person's biological age. But we must recognize that, by virtue of their stage of life, *all* young adults are new followers of Christ. All of them are just beginning that journey of their own free will and independent of their families. All need this kind of investment—from us. And we need this kind of effort to make us strong.

So, what's stopping us? For some of us, we may actually be stuck in stagnation, the state opposite to generativity. Stagnant older adults are, fundamentally, self-absorbed. They focus on what they can get from others, they do not think about the ways they can contribute, and have little interest in being productive or improving themselves. For our purposes, they are notoriously uninterested in young people or are interested in young people only insofar as it can propel their own self-absorption.

But this isn't most of us. Most of us love young people. We are busy and preoccupied, trying to fight the challenges brought by transience, isolation, and distraction ourselves. And we are often also wrestling with the additional insecurities named above.

We are here to be like St Photini,[8] who told her neighbors, "Come see a man who told me all that I ever did. Can this be the Christ?" (John 4:29). Her own life was, unquestionably, somewhat of a mess. She did not understand fully the theological ins-and-outs of what Jesus had told her about the histories and relations of Samaritans and Jews. She wasn't even completely sure who

---

8   St Photini is the name traditionally given to the Samaritan woman Jesus meets at Jacob's Well.

Jesus was. And yet, her response to his loving recognition of her was to go seek out others and share her story of what he had done in her life, exposing herself to a new level of vulnerability (and probably scrutiny) in her community. And for that, we honor her.

Like St Photini, we don't have to have it all figured out to be profoundly helpful to young adults. Instead, we have to be growing ourselves, naming what we're learning or what we learned at key moments, reflecting aloud as we go through life alongside them. Notice what she says—"Come and see," followed by a question, "Can this be the Christ?" Her question is a powerful one—compelling in its humility and its invitation for others to make their own decisions. If we imitate St Photini in this kind of outreach to young adults, we're both vulnerably sharing our own experience of Christ while inviting others to come and learn themselves. As we do this, we'll start learning anew ourselves. As one older team member reflected about his experience working with young adults:

One can always learn more about the faith and continue to evolve as an Orthodox Christian.

Helping form young adults as disciples does not require perfection. It really only requires two things:

- an orientation of coming alongside young adults as we both move towards Christ, treating them as we would wish to be treated; and

- a willingness to listen—to one another and to the Holy Spirit.

If you can activate these two realities in yourself, be ready to be refreshed and inspired by what young adults bring into your life and your parish. You will learn new things—from them and from God—if you take on the discipline of loving young adults in more intentional ways.

Chapter 5

Priests and Parish Leadership: Changing How We Lead Together

Then we will no longer be infants, tossed about by the waves and carried around by every wind of teaching and by the clever cunning of men in their deceitful scheming. Instead, speaking the truth in love, we will in all things grow up into Christ Himself, who is the head. From Him the whole body, fitted and held together by every supporting ligament, grows and builds itself up in love through the work of each individual part.
—*Ephesians 4:14–16*

We've looked at the needs and challenges of young adults and older adults generally, and now we'll turn to the role of formal parish leadership in young adult engagement—priests, parish council members, and other ministry leaders.

We are going to start with priests. The fact that we've left them until now likely surprises many of you—and that is entirely intentional.

We are hoping to correct a somewhat startling but very common assumption, uncovered in pre-Telos focus groups: many, many people believe that their priest and his personality can "make or break" their parish's efforts to engage young adults.

To be more specific, people believe their parish is more likely to attract and retain young adults if their priest is young, charismatic, and energetic. Indeed, it is rare that they name any other factor. And even those other factors they sometimes name—the presence of other young adults and activities for them—are framed as if they are dependent on the priest.

After three years of Telos experimentation across a diversity of parish sizes, cultures, and priests, we are here to declare that this assumption needs to be discarded or, at the very least, seriously nuanced. The majority of the most effective priests in our cohort were not particularly young, nor aggressively charismatic. While they were extremely dedicated to and supportive of young adult ministry, they held their involvement with the young adults in clear balance with all their other responsibilities, often in very large communities. As far as being energetic, the number of tasks they took on personally with regard to young adult ministry were actually relatively few, yet they successfully empowered their teams to be extremely productive.

What they taught us was this: **priests do play a very important role in the spiritual and religious lives of young adults, but they are never the entire story.** Further, it is not their age or their personality that makes the difference, but how young adults experience their priests as leaders and as mentors. *And there is much that lay parish leaders can do to support their priests' efforts.*

What are the hallmarks of an effective priest when it comes to young adult ministry?

Again, not his personality, apparently. Young adults, when given the chance to engage with their priest up close via young adult ministry, are most likely to reflect on the diligence and dedication of their priest, not his personality. Whether a priest is extroverted and gregarious or introverted and quiet seems entirely beside the point; it is his level of investment in the community—his presence with and service to his flock—that young adults name as something that inspires them to want to invest more themselves.

> *I have learned to appreciate my priest and all priests by extension. Being on the Telos leadership team is [a position]…of caring. It will take as much care as you are willing to put into it. I find caring a hard and timely task to do well. By comparison, I look at my priest*

who I know prays for and knows our whole parish community. I find my job difficult to do well. I can only imagine the time and thought that our priest puts into his life and role as our priest. Not only him, but his wife and daughter.

In short, I think about the prayers my priest prays and the thoughts that he must think to be able to care for our parish as well as he does. He provides an example of Godliness to aspire to.

They also showed us that priestly engagement with young adults doesn't have to look the same from priest to priest. **There is great variety in the ways effective priests lead their young adults to be engaged and make a difference.** Some clergy are directly involved in the work of the team while others only peripherally so. Both ways can work well and model serving in accordance with their gifts and capacities.

So the very first thing that wider parish leadership can do to support their priest in his engagement of young adults is to give him the time and space to figure out what young adult ministry in the context of the parish should look like. This will likely encompass him getting to know the young adults who are already involved, inviting them to form a team, helping them discern their roles, and orienting them to parish ministry culture in key ways.

Only if the priest is allowed to do this in a way in which he can express his own authentic gifts and ministry style in a sustainable way will young adults respond in turn with their own authentic gifts and selves. So, parish leaders, don't pressure your priest to "hurry up and do young adult ministry," to host certain kinds of activities immediately, and, in general, monitor how much time he is or isn't spending with the young adults. Both he and your young adults need your patience and your trust as they figure out the shape of their relationship and that of the ministry going forward.

We did find that priests who undertook the following best practices (and parish leaders who supported and/or emulated them) saw impressive results in engagement and productivity from their young adult teams:

First, **effective priests take the time to connect with young adults—to get to know them and their stories.** This probably seems like an obvious first, but it is important to recognize how often parishes inadvertently redirect priests *away* from spending time with young adults to things that might seem more important at that moment, especially in the context of a busy community-wide coffee hour. And how many young adults are going to push their way through the throng of people who "need to talk to Father" to introduce themselves?

So, parish leaders, tune in when there is a new young adult in the room; introduce yourself, get to know them, and then personally connect them to your priest. Prioritize their connection with him over your own business in that moment. You'll be providing both concrete support and an excellent example and young adults will notice.

> *I feel that our Telos team members have a wonderful relationship with our priest.... Having our spiritual guide work so closely with us make it feel that the parish sees [young adult] ministry as something valuable. As well, having the constant support of our priest helps us stay connected and in the loop with all of the activities that our parish are involved in.*

Second, **effective priests "go to bat" for young adults and their ideas.** Clergy who protect young adult agency and ministry experimentation see good results in the kind of enthusiasm and contribution young adults feel energized to bring.

> *The support of our parish priest and presbytera has been instrumental for our [young adult] group. The most recent example is the start of our [young adult] Bible study, which we were given permission to conduct without any strict supervision. Their support is important because it reassures us that we are on the right path*

for creating a strong community of young adults who wish to grow together in Christ, and lead lives that are centered around the church, even though this is not an easy task in our modern world.

Young adults need priests to "go to bat" for them because some of the ways young adults will want to minister to their peers will seem new and different—and possibly threatening to more established groups within the parish, because "we've never done it this way before." Sometimes even something as simple as running a parallel event—even if it draws on a totally different parish demographic—can cause offense or anger. Wise priests know this is a possibility and let young adults try things anyway. They then willingly absorb any challenges to young adults' actions themselves, with dispassion and grace.

Third, when necessary, **effective priests coach young adults in how to navigate the politics of their decisions and be resilient in the face of any community displeasure.** If things get worse before they get better, they fill their young adults with as much love, affirmation, and perspective as possible. They also provide honest feedback on how perhaps young adults can improve their communication or otherwise build their relational capital in the parish.

Fourth, **effective priests affirm young adults as adults!** They model treating young adults as fellow adults and colleagues in meetings, publicly celebrate young adults' successes, thank young adults for their efforts, and invite young adults into wider parish leadership. They do not let young adult contributions be overlooked or attributed to others.

Fifth, in general, **effective priests *energize and equip* young adults without micromanaging them.** They respect young adult agency and capacities, giving them real responsibility in accordance with their gifts, skills, and interests. They know micromanagement tends to backfire, discouraging young adults.

And finally, young adults especially appreciate when **priests spend time with them in a way that helps them deepen their faith,** either by studying with them, answering their questions about Orthodox traditions or teachings, or leading them in prayer or in the context of a retreat.

As proof of this, almost every single Telos team developed some version of "Orthodoxy on Tap" (marketed under several names, including "Brews & Beliefs" and "Orthodoxy on Tapas") in response to young adult requests for a low-key, casual setting in which they could speak with their priest or some other knowledgeable and authoritative person about aspects of the Orthodox tradition or key questions about the faith. These were hosted as stand-alone sessions or as part of a retreat opportunity.

There was also special energy around initiatives in which their priest gave them the necessary know-how to lead spiritual activities on their own—teaching them new skills or introducing them to new resources that help them navigate the sources of the Orthodox tradition together without him, while always having him accessible if they reach an impasse. As one priest shared:

> *Much of what happens spiritually in the lives of the people at [our parish] is up to me, however, that has not been the case with the Telos Team. They want to forge their own path, and it's been rewarding for me to learn to pull back and...actually believe there is such a person as the Holy Spirit who speaks to Christians and beckons them towards growth.*

Launched with the blessing and guidance of their priest, young adults enjoyed leading amongst their peers:

- Bible studies
- Orthodox reading groups (which ranged from reading entire books to single chapters, to short essays or even a single piece of correspondence; the lives of saints, literature by Orthodox greats such as Dostoevsky, and poetic service texts were all popular choices)
- Podcast discussion groups
- Short prayer services that do not require a priest, such as adaptations of the Hours and Akathists

- Selecting, inviting, and hosting a speaker on a spiritual topic

A priest can choose to delegate some of this faith-deepening activity with young adults to others, but young adults consistently express intense appreciation for when the priest himself teaches them and helps them. These sorts of experiences help young adults shrink the gap they have experienced between what they were taught as youth and the new realities of their lives as adults. They feel invested in in a new way by, not just the priest or the parish, but the Church.

I think our young adults feel connected and supported by our parish when we are face to face in some meaningful and engaging discussion with our priest.

Learning more about the faith can sometimes mean young adults see parish life in a new light; this can sometimes bring challenges to parish leadership and the wider community. **Priests can help young adults process these epiphanies with grace and humility.**

One young adult, moving on from her Telos team to serve on her parish council, was startled by how much time was spent by the council on questions of maintaining the church's physical plant—to what felt like the exclusion of almost anything else.

Experiences like these can raise core questions for young adults about the parish's activities or priorities. In the wake of these clarifying moments, they may start asking for changes they believe will lead the parish into greater alignment with its mission, but in ways that can feel challenging to others.

These sorts of "confrontations," between discerned priorities of the gospel and the realities of our lives feel difficult—because they are. But instead of shutting them down, we should welcome them as critically important to the individuals involved and the community as a whole. They are incredible opportunities for growth for everyone if they are received with humility and an openness to repentance and change. They are moments to wrestle with God and one another and not give up.

But how will young adults have these clarifying moments if they are not both exposed to the Gospel and brought into the inner places of church life and leadership? And how will they process them faithfully without companions who can model for them a gracious and forgiving approach to challenges and one another? How will they find new lessons to learn and new reasons to love and respect other parishioners?

> *Throughout the past year I have realized how important it is to not only build a social connection within our team but also how important it is to continue to explore and learn about our Orthodox faith with one another. Our bonds as a team have strengthened this year and I don't believe that is just because of time but because of the intention we have had in building our team's culture.*
>
> *I have gained a deeper respect for the people in leadership roles here and the work they do to build a community where people can show up and plug in quickly.*

Young adults need the scriptures, they need the lives of the saints, the prayers of the Church, the living example of their older brothers and sisters in Christ, and the holy wisdom that animates them all. And their priest can help them navigate these, welcoming them into the real topography of Orthodox Christian life and community—its ups and downs, its possibilities and challenges. And he can do it not as a disembodied talking head of the Internet, but as a person who is deeply interested in them, who will answer their questions in a coffee shop on Friday afternoon, listen to their struggles in confession on a Saturday evening and then feed them—in faith and love—on Sunday morning.

All of these best practices are ways that **young adults feel actively invested in by a priest**. And when young adults feel loved by priests, they in turn build healthy community amongst themselves, with the rest of the parish, and become leaders in their own right. Young adults who transition to other parish leadership often contribute substantially, their work rebounding to the priest and the rest of the community in extremely encouraging ways.

This process is accelerated and deepened when lay leaders in the parish take up the same sense of responsibility towards young adults that we seem to universally expect from our priests. We've already spoken of how we ourselves will grow personally when we willingly enter into discipling relationships with young adults…but our parishes will grow and change too.

How can parish leaders support their priest in this work and these processes? Firstly, by freeing him to be able to do them. What we are describing are critical pastoral tasks—and yet, somehow, because they are for young adults, they are sometimes ranked as less important than other tasks that the priest has on his plate. And secondly, parish leaders can recognize the patterns their community may tend towards when confronted with change and come alongside the priest in smoothing the path for young adult ideas and efforts whenever necessary.

What does this look like? Speaking up graciously—at meetings or in private conversations—in support of time the priest spends with young adults, particular new ideas, trial efforts in general, of learning through failure, and of the young adults themselves is a huge help and something every parish leader can do more of.

Further, when **lay leaders join their priest in intentionally being gracious and encouraging towards young adults, the efforts of the priest are magnified way beyond what he could achieve on his own.** When other parish leaders freely offer hospitality to young adults, a sounding board, and encourage resilience in hard moments or frustrating seasons, share what in their own faith gives them the motivation to keep going— "ministering to the ministers"—young adults finally begin to believe that they are really an equal part of the Body of Christ.

> *After this year of Telos work it's clear to me that young adults need their own unique space in the life of the Church but they cannot be isolated from the wider parish life and community. This year we have made many more connections within the Parish Council and also with other ministries within the Church and that has strengthened our sense of belonging and our purpose. In many ways the young adult ministry is more active and more people within the community*

> know what we are up to and therefore more connections have been made and have added a lot of value to our year.

Let's face it: parish relationships can be difficult and young adult lives are already full of significant challenges and transitions. When older adults are attuned to these dynamics and offer real, concrete support, then young adults' energy and attentiveness to their ministry and to one another increases.

Even more fruitful: when **parish leaders adopt a stance of learning alongside their young adults.** Telos work is not about young adults engaging young adults *instead* of older adults doing it; it's about how the whole community learns how to be more welcoming and then puts that learning into practice.

And suddenly, parish leaders have learned how to operate and oversee ministry in a way that focuses on connection, creates community that energizes, allows for agency, and deepens faith. And they can use what they have learned in young adult ministry, but also beyond young adult ministry, in all areas of parish life. And they'll find that parish life takes on a wonderful new feel. As one parish priest reflected:

> ...if I thought more about the best experience with the Telos group, it would have been after the Bridegroom Orthros on Tuesday night. I was exhausted already, and after I closed everything up, I just went and sat in our lobby—waiting for people to leave so I could lock up. There were about 12 of our YAs in the narthex, chatting. And four "old adults." They could not see me. It was such a beautiful <u>sound</u>: voices, laughing, love. I got to sit there for probably 15 minutes, listening, as if to a symphony.

Slowly but surely, we will transform our parish cultures into something more broadly welcoming and deeply satisfying, into symphonies. We will renew our inner life in a way that will cause us to turn around and look at each other with new eyes and then look outwards toward our neighbors. We will let go of the fear that we might lose our beloved parishes and our young adults...and by holding them much more lightly, we might just be inviting them to explode with new life.

Chapter 6

Becoming A Vibrant Parish: Finding Our Telos Together

By this all people will know that you are my disciples: if you have love for one another. — John 13:35

Let's step back to the vineyard where we began. We want to leave you with a vision of what learning to love young adults can do for your parish as a whole organism—if you let it. **If you love your parish and want it to thrive, cultivate young adult engagement as one of your key priorities.**

We are not advocating for this because young adults are more important than anyone else in your congregation. There is much wrong with the way that American culture glorifies young adulthood and its capacities, often at the expense of other stages of life. But, to be brutally honest, there is also something deeply disordered and disordering about how so many of our parishes have devolved to the point of ignoring young adults. Unique deficits require uniquely intense solutions…and we promise you will find young adults a particularly productive point to which you can apply your efforts for parish growth and renewal.

Why? **Because learning to love young adults is, essentially, learning to love.** It's learning to garden, to cultivate with intention. It's learning to no longer take anyone or anything for granted. To track weather conditions and water intentionally, instead of assuming it will rain. To not assume they'll find nourishment, what to pick and when, but to feed them and then teach them to harvest alongside us. To not assume they'll find people in the parish who will care about them, but to become the people in the parish who care about them.

Of course, in Christ we are meant to love everyone, not just young adults—but telling ourselves that rarely results in us actually doing it. Taking on the love of young adults as a discipline, however, is an excellent way to train ourselves in a new level of attentiveness, in openness to and care of others, in Christian hospitality—which we can then extend to anyone.

And young adults themselves can often lead the way and remind us how to offer hospitality. In the natural course of their lives, they are constantly being put in the position of having to engage with new people. As one priest shared:

> Several times this year, we've had young adults move to the area, for work or for internships at the hospital. I usually contact these new "members" and tell them about the church programming, and perhaps meet with them once or twice. But in several instances, the [young adult ministry] has really stepped up to make these young adults feel welcome in ways that the church—before Telos—could not. Or did not.

If we empower young adults to provide community that energizes, and give them access to agency and the spiritual food and encouragement they need to deepen their faith—young adults will love and welcome others and they'll teach us how to love and welcome others.

> I've learned that I have so much work to do on becoming a loving and welcoming person. The Telos team at [our parish] has gone so far above and beyond any group I've ever seen to make newcomers feel welcome.

> I am inspired as an adviser to see our young adults bring new people to the faith. Seeing a young adult chrismated into the faith was a special moment.

Young adults will help us see one another anew, reminding us of the richness that we already possess. As an older adult shared:

> … *"Life is a journey of meeting new people." I have been a member [of our parish]… for over 25 years and still did not know many of my fellow parishioners. Being part of Telos has introduced me to some amazing people.*

The COVID-19 pandemic provoked many epiphanies, including a realization of how precious in-person Christian community is, but also how taken for granted and how fragile. We were all asleep in the sameness of our routines and suddenly we were all shaken awake. We were all forced to ask ourselves: what is the Church—the *ekklesia*—when we are not believers gathered together?

The parishes who answered that question best were those who looked through the lens the other way: what is the Church when we believers *are* gathered together? What's most important? What makes us the Church? And what does that mean we need now?

Whatever else is distinctive and wonderful and life-giving about Orthodoxy—and there is so much—the chief answer to the question "What makes us the Church?" should be "Christ's love"—for God, for one another, for the world. Because when Christ's love is missing, young adults find little reason to stay in our parishes. **Because everything else, in our world of abundance, they can find anywhere else.** In the words of one young adult:

> *I have always been involved in the church, I was [formally educated in theology], I do iconography professionally, I study scriptures on my own time… but something that Telos has shown me is how important it is for a community to make sure that its young adults stay connected with each other and have Christ centered discussions with each other. From Telos I have learned how important it is to become closer with my church family. We are all walking down the same path, and it is important to not let each other feel that we are walking alone.*

So what do we need now to integrate young adults? Christ's love. Christ's love is the Church's identity and it is also our vocation. There is meant to be no division between these two things. We sometimes fall into the temptation of believing that loving one another is what we do when our labor is done; after we have done the hard work of keeping the parish afloat, then we will celebrate, love, and enjoy one another. But young adults in Telos, through trial and error, through successes and failures, grew into the understanding that in the Church, our love and our labor must be one—otherwise, we are not living into being the Church.

> *"Therefore comfort each other and edify one another, just as you also are doing," (1 Thessalonians 5:11) [Our young adult ministry] truly believes in encouraging and motivating one another. 1 Thessalonians 5:11 is a reminder that when Christ came to console and encourage the people, He set an example to us all of how to continually support each other through love and acceptance. We believe in uplifting and helping each other, and we do this by assigning roles, delegating tasks, organizing events and meetups, by recognizing when someone is struggling and offering our help, and also by praising each other for our achievements. This verse goes beyond our [ministry] team; by practicing this with the members of our own team, we have learned the importance of spreading our love and support to all who need it.*

They also learned that when love and labor become hard, as they did during the pandemic, it is not time to give up. It is time, instead, for creativity, flexibility, even ambition.

> *Young adults play a very important role in the life of the Church. They often bring creativity and are much more adaptive than some of its older members. In this sense, young adults play an important role in sustaining the Church during difficult times.*

They have taught us not to give up either. And in their not giving up, there have been moments they've become living illustrations of the words of St Paul (1 Timothy 4:12): "Let no one look down on your youthfulness, but rather in speech, conduct, love, faith, and purity, show yourself an example of those who believe." As one parish priest shared:

> *The new [young adult ministry] ... has been a beacon of light in the parish by 1) being present at services, 2) welcoming visitors in ways that the general parish does not, and 3) sustaining programs on their own during the quarantine.*

Young adults, engaged respectfully and well, will bring your parish hope and necessary challenge. In relationship with them, you'll reencounter all the foundational questions of faith and the critical elements of parish life—and if you've grown weak, you'll have the chance to grow strong. You will be given the opportunity, as individuals and as a parish, to begin again.

Find your telos; find out what your parish, your corner of the vineyard, was created to bring forth. Labor alongside one another—young adults and older adults together—in such a way that you might be known for your good works—your love, faith, service, and patient endurance. And may your last works be greater than your first.

A Summary of Reflective Prompts

Remember Your Own Story

Think about your own young adulthood. How did you find your place in the Church?

Who were important influences and support as you searched for that place, such that you are grateful for them today? What did they do for you, what did they say to you?

Get to Know Your Young Adults

Set yourself the goal of meeting a new young adult this Sunday—or learning more about one you may have already met. Some simple introductory questions might include:

- How they found the parish and what brought them here;
- What they do for a living or what they are studying and what they love about it;
- Where they grew up, and similarities and differences with their own parish, if they grew up in one, whether it was Orthodox or not.

If you already know them, a simple question like, "How are you doing?", "how is work going?", or "how was your week?" can open up a whole area that they'd love to talk about or process. Above all, allow your approach to have the warmth with which you might reach out to a beloved niece or nephew.

Invest in Young Adults, Building Them Up

Ask your priest to identify concrete, specific ways you can support him having time and bandwidth to connect to the young adults in your community.

Does your parish have a line item in its budget for young adult ministry? If not, what would it take to add one?

Concurrent with any questions around budget, review and encourage your parish's active thoughtfulness around investing in young adult leadership. Are young adults given the agency, encouragement, and support to spend your parish's young adult budget on a wide variety of activities to meet their needs—including fellowship, opportunities to serve and deepen their faith, and intergenerational relationship building?

Cultivate Generativity in Yourself

What young adults are you sharing your life with right now—your time, your expertise, your hospitality, your story? How can you continue to build up that relationship?

What young adult are you helping to cultivate in their faith, sense of purpose and belonging in the Church, even in small ways? Can you think about ways you could expand that investment?

Which young adult can you pray and light a candle for this Sunday?

Partner with Young Adults

Does your parish council have young adults on it? If it doesn't, how can it lay the groundwork to change that?

Are young adults active in other sorts of ministries in your parish? If not, what would it take to help these ministries invite and welcome young adults?

Has your parish ever enjoyed an event or series completely planned and directed by young adults? What kind of vision and preparation would it take to get your parish to that amazing demonstration of young adult leadership?

Outreach Beyond Your Parish

What more can your parish do to let young adults in your town or city know that your parish exists and that you would welcome them? Who else in your parish should you talk to about these ideas?

Is there a young adult who doesn't attend your parish whom you could reach out to and invite to coffee, lunch, or an event at your parish?

About the Authors

The real authors of this book were all the individuals on the Telos teams. Without their efforts, there would be no story to tell. To that end, we are profoundly grateful for the pilot parish communities who shared insights with us from 2017–2021, through three cycles of ministry design and testing, COVID and all.

St Athanasius Orthodox Church, Nicholasville, KY (OCA)

St Barbara Greek Orthodox Church, Orange, CT (GOA)

St George Greek Orthodox Church, Chicago, IL (GOA)

Holy Trinity Greek Orthodox Church, Dallas, TX (GOA)

Holy Trinity Greek Orthodox Church, Pittsburgh, PA (GOA)

St John Orthodox Church, Memphis, TN (AOCNA)

St John the Wonderworker Orthodox Church, Atlanta, GA (OCA)

St Mary Orthodox Church, Cambridge, MA (AOCNA)

Protection of the Holy Mother of God Orthodox Church, Falls Church, VA (OCA)

St Nektarios Greek Orthodox Church, Charlotte, NC (GOA)

Resurrection Greek Orthodox Church, Castro Valley, CA (GOA)

St Sophia Greek Orthodox Church, Syracuse, NY (GOA)

Did these communities work out every detail of vibrant and healthy young adult ministry? Of course not. Did they venture bravely ahead of us all to discover and mark a trail? A thousand times, yes. With their help, we now have a map—rough and in need of additional refinement—that guides in building parish-based ministries that honor both the timeless truths of the Orthodox tradition and the realities of young adults in our time.

As for those of us entrusted to witness and document their work....

Ann Mitsakos Bezzerides, has served as Director of the Office of Vocation & Ministry at Hellenic College Holy Cross since 2003 and is now also Executive Director of CrossRoad Institute Inc (CRI). She has a BA in English from Middlebury College, an MDiv from St Vladimir's Orthodox Theological Seminary, and a PhD in Religion and Education from Boston College. She and her husband, Dr Vassilios Bezzerides, have three sons and live in Brookline, MA. Her love for young adults grows naturally from her love for the alumni of the CrossRoad 10-day high school summer institute—whom she knows are looking for vibrant parish homes and ways to serve!

Jenny Haddad Mosher served as Director of the Telos Project from 2017 to 2022, and now supports all of CRI's programming as Director of Research & Educational Design. She has a BA in History from Yale College, an MAR in Scripture from Yale Divinity School, an MTh in Systematic Theology & Ethics from St Vladimir's Orthodox Theological Seminary, and a PhD in Religion and Education from Union Theological Seminary in the City of New York. She and her husband, Fr Joshua Mosher, live in Durham, CT, with her mother, their three young adult sons, and a (seemingly) never ending stream of their sons' young adult friends. Somehow there is always enough room at the dinner table(s) for everyone.

Utmost gratitude to additional individuals and organizations who imagined, supported, encouraged, and expanded this work: Chris Coble and Chanon Ross of Lilly Endowment for asking such provocatively hard questions and then giving generously the tools to try to figure out responses; Hellenic College Holy Cross for understanding the importance of this kind of research work for the life of the Church; Hellenic Foundation Chicago for requesting and funding an extension project, TelosGamma; Anna Colis Kallis for being our brilliant ministry collaborator and leader of TelosGamma, piloting critical revisions of the process; Saints Constantine and Helen Greek Orthodox Church in Cambridge, MA, for being willing to take the project to a new level and host our new Telos Center, a ministry lab for all these ideas; the board and advisors of CrossRoad Institute, stalwart and hopeful in focusing us on the critical nature of this work; and the incredible young adults who piloted "Telos POP" during a global pandemic and shone a light on what is possible with agency, resilience, faithfulness, and hope.

Orthodox parishes must engage and shape upcoming leaders today, not tomorrow. We need to be willing to come alongside and invest heavily in young adults now, seeing it as one of the most critical things we do. It's what they need, what we need, and what our parishes need if we will all grow strong in Christ.

—Michael Hyatt
New York Times bestselling author

The five-year Telos Project has resulted in this fine compilation of ideas for young adult ministry. Described in the prologue as "a quick read and simple," it is that and much more. First of all, one will rarely find such honest and heartfelt reflections as those communicated by the young adults who participated in the project. The "best practices" offered can easily be reproduced in parishes wanting to actively encourage young adults to engage more deeply in their Orthodox Christian faith. Yet I find myself thinking that many of the needs, concerns, and desires expressed by the young adults in this book are not unlike those of older adults, many of whom also feel disconnected and are searching for love, truth, connection, and ultimately for Jesus Christ. Therefore, I believe that this is much more than a helpful manual for young adult ministry. By considering the perspectives and practical recommendations of the young adults quoted in this book, parishes may become better attuned to engaging adults of all ages. In this way, the young adults of the Telos Project have led the way in revealing effective ways to welcome, encourage, and involve young adults and older adults alike, toward the telos of a deeper relationship with Jesus Christ — and with one another — in His Holy Orthodox Church.

—Dr Paraskevè (Eve) Tibbs
Christian Education Ministry Lead
Greek Orthodox Metropolis of San Francisco

Written to be a "quick, simple, and provocative" read, Find Your Telos prompts full consideration of how to engage young adults in the dynamic life of the parish family. Although the authors provide thoughtful insights into the modern young adult experience, Telos is not just another program or curriculum for young adults. Rather, it is a framework for thinking about and implementing ministry that actually benefits all generations in the parish through deeply meaningful relationships and purpose. Find Your Telos is for everyone who wants an energized, vibrant, and relevant parish, building up the body of Christ and walking with all on the path to salvation.

—Randa Anderson, PhD
President
Orthodox Christian Association of Medicine,
Psychology, and Religion

In this book, Ann Mitsakos Bezzerides and Jenny Haddad Mosher have provided a compass and a road map for the journey we should all be on to engage young adults more fully with our Faith and the life of the Church. Their insights are clear, compelling, and grounded in both research and experience. The challenge they provide for us is one we should all embrace.

—Tim Tassopoulos
Former President and COO of Chick-fil-A

An alarming condition has beset our young people in recent years, and although there are some notable exceptions, many in our Church seem either to misunderstand the problem or to be at a loss as to how to address it. This wonderful and important book provides both diagnosis and cure for what ails us. Theologically grounded and informed by current research in human development, the book is the product of years and years of successful and innovative experience in youth and young adult ministry. It is, thus, written from the ground up. It also has a clear and engaging style that reads effortlessly. It should be studied not only by clergy and lay ministers, but also by parents and by young people themselves.

—Rev George Parsenios, PhD
Professor of New Testament
Holy Cross Greek Orthodox School of Theology

The new Telos book is a captivating and transforming book for everyone who reads it. A quick and easy read, it provides the reader with renewed energy coupled with wisdom that tells how young adults can contribute significantly to Orthodox parishes and how our Orthodox parishes can become more Christ-centered through inclusion of the life-blood of our young adults. I love it.

—Dr Albert S Rossi
Director of Counseling & Psychological Services
St Vladimir's Orthodox Theological Seminary